HYPOTHETICALLY SPEAKING

OUT LOUD

If "X" Were True

What Would It

Mean For "Y"

MICHELLE R. JACKSON-MCCOY, PH.D.

Paperback ISBN 978-0-9727949-2-3
Ebook ISBN 978-0-9727949-1-6

Printed in the United States of America.

Editorial Design: Julia Bramer
Cover Design: David Ter-Avanesyan
Cover Photograph: Angela Cigarroa

First Edition

For media inquiries, speaking engagements, and signed copies:

drmichellejm.com/contact

Also By Dr. Michelle R. Jackson-McCoy

FOR I AM

This book is dedicated to one of the most amazing and influential women I have ever known. Her name is Ruby Ann Jackson. She brought me into this world, taught me about this world, and set me free to discover every amazing feature about this world while always standing near. I am grateful for so much so often. She was not only the one that taught me how to spread my wings; she was the one that told me I have wings. Now she has a beautiful, shiny, new pair of her own. I love you, and I miss you dearly.

There is a quote by Prince Harry that best sums up what I feel in this moment. He said:

> *"I hope that a lot of my mother's talents are shown in a lot of the work that I do."*

THE VAULT

THE VAULT is where I have placed a few of the pictures, quotes, and thoughts that were meaningful to me as I was writing this book. I have decided to share them with you.

THE VAULT IS AT:
drmichellejm.com

To the Reader

The stories in this book are true. Although the incidents you will read about are of a particular child, adult, family, or me, these stories represent millions of individuals from every walk of life and every corner of the world.

About the Names

The names of some people in this book have been changed. The names of others are intentionally revealed because I desire to speak their names out loud. My desire is to give credit to "amazing!"

Contents

Thinking

Out Loud

One:

Finally, I Am Ready To Speak

With every experience, you alone are
painting your own canvas, thought
by thought, choice by choice.

— Oprah Winfrey

We wake up every morning with something as powerful as a voice and a choice. Every morning presents a new opportunity to ask, "What am I doing with mine?" But whether you consciously pose the question, consciously ignore the question, or don't consider the question at all, it continues to be asked. The question does not require your permission in order to exist. With or without your permission, it continues to pose itself to each of us every day. At the end of each day we all answer.

My continual effort to discover my own version of answers that I can live with is what led me to the equation: if "X" were true, what would it mean for "Y"? This is the essential question I am asking on every page of every chapter within this book. Each chapter is a type of mathematical equation. It's just a little harder to see the math because the equation is presented in the most familiar and disarming form—as stories.

Writing stories, or more accurately stated, writing in general, can be a difficult and draining process until you are ready to speak.

Speaking out can be a difficult and draining process until you understand what you have to say. Knowing what you have to say is frustrating until you can find someone who is willing to listen. Having someone that will listen can be difficult and draining if you do not feel you are in the company of someone who cares.

This reflects how I felt in the beginning stages of writing this book. I started with having too much to say and being not quite ready to speak. When I felt ready to speak, or at least thought I was ready to speak, I could not figure out how to get it all to make sense outside of my own head. Then I sat at my computer trying to figure out what people would want to hear. That was terribly frustrating, because how could I figure out what people wanted to hear if I could not figure out to whom I was speaking? Well, as my grandmother would say when she didn't feel like filling in the details of a story, "long story short," it was one heck of a writer's block and lasted over a decade.

Fast forward to today, and I cannot stop writing. The words are falling out of me. What has taken me so long to get here? Maybe I just tired of trying to figure out how to verbally package my message. Maybe I just got older and started caring less about a lot of things that used to matter, and more about some of the things that mattered less. All I know is that amid my many years of confusion, I am now clear on one thing—I could not have finished this book a minute sooner. I guess some would say, I finally "arrived"! Whatever that means and wherever we are arriving once we get there, I do not know the exact location, but through this journey, I have discovered it is somewhere inside me.

Today, I am not only ready to speak, I understand what I am saying and am crystal clear on to whom I am speaking. I am talking to everybody! By using stories, my intent was to make it easier to see the problem(s) that need to be solved, addressed, or, at a minimum, acknowledged. That also means I am hoping the stories will help make it easier for you to find your own versions of meaningful solutions for those moments when what once existed as a hypothetical in your life arrives at your doorstep and becomes your reality.

Let's talk a little more about what is "X." "X" could be a behavior, attitude, mindset, human condition, etc. It is the outcome/summation that results each day from the ways you elect to use your voice and the ways in which you wield your privilege of choice. "X" is the summation that answers for you and the rest of the world the question, "What am I doing with mine?" Essentially, "X" is where you discover what you feel, believe, and value, which, at its core, is what defines your answer to the perpetual question, "What am I doing with mine?" The cumulative effect of your answers over time is what informs and becomes "your story." What you will read in this book are my stories and the stories of those that have crossed my path. They are honest accounts of our "X" and how we have, have not impacted, or desperately hope to impact "Y."

So, if "X" represents your voice (when you speak, whether you speak, how you speak, and what you speak about) and choice (all the many choices you make in the course of a day—whether to care, share, uplift, tear down, ignore, or celebrate)—, then "Y" represents all the ways the world is impacted by your "X."

As you read the stories contained in this book, keep these few points in mind: First, this equation is not one-sided. We are not only solving for "Y." It goes both ways. We are also solving for "X."

Secondly, our position within the equation is interchangeable. Sometimes we are "X" and sometimes we are "Y." In other words, sometimes you are the one that can change the circumstance, and sometimes you are "Y," the one being impacted by someone else's voice and choice. The "Y" is the person(s) affected by the circumstance. In algebraic equations, "X" and "Y" are referred to as the independent and dependent variables. In this equation, "Y" is the dependent variable. "Y" is dependent on what happens with "X." In contrast, "X" is the independent variable. As "X" changes, "Y" changes.

Third, it is not always just "X" and "Y." There is always something influencing people and circumstances, although we might not notice this infinite chain of variables influencing the equation. There could be a "Z" influencing "X" or a "W" influencing "Y." Anything your mind, emotions, or life experience can conjure up could potentially be a "Z" or a "W." It could be a feeling, occurrence, money, or another person. Regardless of what it is or who it is, they all have different magnitudes but equal significance in the equation. Typically, we manage this infinite chain of variables by primarily focusing on what we feel we can control.

As you read the stories in this book, what you will notice is how we take different pathways to get to our "X." Sometimes it requires us to bring something (addition). Sometimes, instead of bringing something, we choose to significantly expand what already exists in that space (multiplication). Sometimes we remove or take something away (subtraction), and sometimes we choose to divide. The point is, just like we have the power to choose "X," we always have the power to change "X," and we are all responsible for our own equation. Oftentimes, our greatest challenge is not that we fail to function responsibly with our "X." Our greatest challenge is remaining cognizant of the fact that we all have an "X" and that "X" matters.

As it is with everything, there is always a downside. The same is true for equations or, more generally, with math. The downside is that math forces you to view results based upon the dichotomy of "right" and "wrong." This can be a challenging barometer when the variables involve human life.

Speaking hypothetically, what if we changed the system and instead evaluated life based upon impact and consequences that resulted from our voice and choice or lack thereof? Then our evaluation would give more consideration to the cost of repair, like we do when we encounter a car accident. You would be evaluating your "X" based upon whether there was damage and the extent of the damage your "X" caused for "Y." Cost would be based upon what would be required to make the repairs, and additional cost would be added for any pain and suffering. But, of course, that is just me hypothetically speaking out loud.

In writing this book, I began by giving myself permission to think out loud, which is what you are reading now. In the next section I take a moment to reflect out loud through a series of true stories. In the end I give myself permission to imagine hope and speculate—out loud.

Hypothetically Speaking Out Loud is a collection of thoughts, hopes, considerations, and true stories. As each unfolds, it will take you on a journey into some of the darkest and brightest times in my life and the lives of those that have walked with me or have crossed my path. They are inspiring and sometimes painful accounts of those with whom I have experienced empowering moments, lessons learned, missed opportunities, and simple celebrations. It is a book of "awakenings," with each one centered on two concepts: One concept is represented in the equation, "If 'X' were true, what would it mean for 'Y'?" The second concept is represented in the idea, "What if our hypotheticals came true?"

What if you could wake up one day and not only hope for better days, but believe you have the power to make those days a reality for yourself and others. To feel passion and suddenly realize you discovered purpose in the process. To be awakened enough to see that some of the greatest miracles happen in the smallest of moments. Each story of each awakening in this book is a reminder of the power of one person to make a difference. This book is a reminder that such power is in us all. It is the power to reach, rise, radiate, inspire, affirm, and even rescue sometimes others and sometimes ourselves.

As I asked myself why I was compelled to write this book, the answer came swiftly. I believe there is good in each of us. But, after some thought, I realized that this book was not written because I believe we are good. This book was written because I believe we are unknowingly powerful.

As you read through the pages, I hope you will enjoy both the stories and the conversation I am having with you. For the first time, I am using a book to speak out loud in a very personal manner. It feels so good. What makes it feel amazing is: 1) The thoughts and feelings no longer exist only inside me, and 2) I have grown enough and lived enough that I no longer feel the need to shout. My volume is my form of celebration. It is my expression of freedom. Out loud is not a statement of volume. It simply means "outside of me." The word "hypothetical," well, that is just me giving myself permission to speculate. To explore the what-ifs and the if-thens of life. Thus, I have written a book that is driven by an equation that addresses both. This book represents my exploration of my own suppositions regarding hypotheticals.

One final note I feel compelled to mention. As you move through the stories, you will encounter my experiences with individuals that almost the entire planet will know due to their fame, and you will encounter individuals that no one will recognize at all. The names and fame are irrelevant. What matters are the moments.

I hope you will see that my stories are actually your stories, because there is some part of each story that is *our* story. What you will experience on each page are simple, complicated, wonderfully joyous, painfully heart-tugging moments in my life and in the lives of others. Moments that define my "X" and theirs, when we are presented with the opportunity to either watch, walk away, or touch the world.

Reflecting

Out Loud

Two:

In
Search
of a Cure

Success is not final; failure is
not fatal: it is the courage to
continue that counts.

— Winston S. Churchill

Finally! I never thought this day would come! That was my thought at the time. After so many years of schooling, I finally was so close to finishing, as signaled by my advisor's conversation with me regarding completing the internship requirement for my Ph.D. I was preparing to go out into the world and begin making a difference: my favorite form of "X."

But that is not what felt new and exciting to me. Making a difference and impacting lives is the air I breathe. What felt new and exciting was the fact that this time I would be going out and making a difference with a few new letters behind my name—"Michelle Jackson, ABD." When you are in a Ph.D. program and have completed all your coursework and passed the comprehensive exam, those initials are like a badge of honor. They stand for "All But Dissertation." I laugh as I look back on it. After a few weeks, the newness of the title wore off. My classmates and I would tease each other because, in reality ABD just felt like, "All

But Done!"

As I was working to secure an internship, I was so excited to receive an invitation to intern at the UCLA Neuropsychiatric Institute. I was honored. They scheduled for me to meet with a woman I will call Dr. Kimble. She would be supervising me. I arrived at her office. We were cordial, but professionalism abounded. She asked me a few questions. Apparently, my answers were sufficient, because very shortly thereafter she began showing me videotapes of the types of clients I would be working with as part of a major study.

The monitor turned on, and there was a middle-aged woman sitting in a chair in an almost empty room with bare, pale yellow walls. Her hair was neat and modestly styled, and she was nicely dressed, calm, and articulate. You could hear the voice of someone asking her a question, but they were off camera. As she was talking, different personalities began to manifest, and she would introduce them as they appeared. They had different names. The woman suffered from schizophrenia.

I remember my heart aching for her as I watched. What do you do when your brain paints a completely different picture of reality? A picture so vivid and real that you are convinced it is truth, but yet it is only your truth. Not another person on the planet sees what you see. Nor will they be able to validate your version of reality.

I pray we continue to elevate the importance of mental health. All forms of these debilitating disorders, from depression to PTSD to everything in-between and beyond. Those that suffer are as human as you and me, and all too often they suffer in silence. They routinely use every ounce of their energy just to get through a day without a major incident. They must continue to matter.

After coming home and contemplating where I wanted to spend the next year of my life, I found myself grateful for the opportunity at the Neuropsychiatric Institute, but I was slow to accept the offer. My heart was guiding me in a different direction.

I have always had a tremendous passion for helping those that are labeled "high-risk" and "hard-to-reach." That generally led me to low-income, inner-city communities. I guess it makes sense that my heart would lead me in that direction. After all, I was born and raised in a low-income, inner-city community. I was one of the numbers in those statistics you frequently hear quoted. But from the inside, all those labels and statistics looked different, because the numbers had names that were attached to people. Not just people: They were attached to people I knew, loved, and who shaped me into the woman I am today.

Those labels and numbers are attached to Mrs. Jean Davis. I always have called and still do call her "Miss Jean." She has been married all the years I have known her. But she has never flinched or questioned my use of that prefix and never failed to answer when I called. When I was a little girl, in our culture, it was disrespectful to call an adult by their first name without putting something in front of it like "Mr.," "Mrs.," "Aunt," or, in my case, "Miss." It is a statement of respect and honor for the adults who were typically viewed as warriors fighting for opportunities and freedoms that many of them would never live to enjoy. There was also an unspoken recognition that times were hard for people of color and that surviving to see your forties, fifties, sixties and up was an accomplishment all by itself that deserved a statement of commendation.

As I think of Miss Jean and those statistics, I realize how much data is missing. The statistics do not show how hard she and her husband worked to send all three of their sons to private school. The statistics do not show all of Miss Jean's civic involvement, and I doubt you will find any calculations for the percentage of my success that can be attributed to her sheer willingness to take the time to care. That is the significance of the equation in this book. The "X" in my equation (if "X" were true, what would it mean for

"Y"?) also accounts for variables that are not on our radar or are outside of our view, yet they are impacting "Y."

At the time of my childhood, Miss Jean was the only woman my family knew that had finished college. We thought she knew everything, not realizing that in college you major in one, or maybe two topics. I never knew and still do not know Miss Jean's major. All I remember is that I never asked her a question for which she did not go and find the answer. I know that every paper I typed was on Miss Jean's typewriter that she would hand to us over the backyard fence, where eventually her husband, Mr. Davis, built a gate for convenience. As the years went on and time, elements, and gravity began to wear on the old fence, Mr. Davis built another fence and included a gate! It was the most normal thing in the world to hear my mother end a phone conversation with Miss Jean saying, "Okay, I'll meet you at the gate!" or, "Tell Michelle I gave Jimmy [one of Miss Jean's sons] the World Encyclopedia 'K' that she asked for. He's at the gate!"

Miss Jean was a wife and the mother of three very athletic and very active boys, worked full-time, and was involved in whatever made the city of Compton better. She had a busy life, but I cannot remember one time when she was too busy for me. Not one time! It is so important that the Miss Jeans of the world continue to live on. Not that they would live forever, but that we would recognize the importance of picking up the mantle and carrying it forward from where they left off.

My mother was very protective of her children and very particular about who entered our family circle. What my mother shared with Miss Jean was something special. They started out together as young mothers. That relationship lasted with the same unwavering love and respect for one another for over a half-century. It lasted until the day my mother took her last breath. When my mother passed away a few years ago, she was one year from turning ninety.

Then there were those individuals in my neighborhood who may not have shared the intimacy of the back gate, but who did not hesitate to sow into me and others whatever powerful seed they had. Mrs. Thelma Wright comes to mind. She would always tell me to stay in school as she watched from her screen door. At the time, I was a young girl in elementary school. It never dawned on me to leave school. So, at the time I was not quite sure why, when I would ride my bike past her house and she would hear the rhythmic squeak of my front bicycle wheel, she would holler from the screen door, "Girl! You stay in school!" Now, having the benefit of time, I understand that Mrs. Thelma was making sure I did not connect with what might have been referred to at the time as the "wrong crowd."

Somehow, from her screen door, she knew everything that was happening in the neighborhood: the good, the bad, and the ugly. We never understood how she had so much information, but my mother loved when Mrs. Thelma shared it with her! From my vantage point, I only heard my mother's comments, given that the speaker phone had not been invented yet. I would hear long periods of silence while my mother just listened, and Mrs. Thelma would fill her ear with news. I knew it was juicy just by watching my mother's expression shift from surprise to being blown away. All I would hear my mother say is a stream of, "No!" "Girl, you got to be kidding me!" "No, he didn't!" "She did what?"

But Mrs. Thelma believed I had potential and wanted to make sure I had a chance to make it out of the community. It is funny looking back on it. We talked about making it out as though there was a wall around our community that prevented us from leaving. You could be one street away from a completely different lifestyle. There were no walls, just policies, procedures, pre-judgments, a lack of capital, and sometimes our own mindset that frequently made the thought of leaving the hood a distant dream. But at least we kept dreaming.

In my hood, when one got out, it was a victory for everybody, as they hoped and prayed you would remember the ones that remained. The matriarch warriors in the neighborhood would think, "Maybe from the outside that one can help us, help tell the truth about our story." It is hard living, but it was home. Well, this girl did remember, and I still remember.

I have brought millions of dollars in programs and resources back to the community. And every chance I get, I let the world know, not only am I from Compton, California, but I am a product of the Mrs. Jeans, Mrs. Thelmas, Ms. Carrie Marks, and more. I have unmeasurable love for these strong warriors, some of whom are no longer with us except in spirit, and others who are still just a phone call away.

So, I thanked UCLA, turned down their invitation, and accepted an internship in the department of psychiatry at a hospital located in the heart of the hood. Excited and relieved that the decision was made, I began to prepare for my first day at the place that had now become my platform for impacting "Y."

In the days leading up to my first day on the job, I had sophomoric dreams. I was convinced I was going to change the world. What I knew was that I had a heart for the people and believed my passion would guide me toward making a positive difference in their lives. I was feasting on the words of Albert Einstein, who said, "The world is a dangerous place, not because of those who do evil, but because of those who look on and do nothing." I was determined not to fall into the "do nothing" category!

The day of my internship arrived. I went to the hospital to report in and was met by my supervisor, who we will refer to as Dr. Jordon Dandridge. How happy I was to see him. Dr. Dandridge and I had worked together on a research project a few years earlier. We had interacted well as researchers. This would be our first time working together as clinicians. He knew I was at the top of my class in research and had no doubt that my performance as an intern would be no less in quality than what he had experienced with me in the past.

After a few minutes of small talk, he began to describe the history of the hospital and to explain how the department of psychiatry was structured. We talked as we walked. He began showing me the patient admission and treatment process.

On the second floor, we arrived at a set of large, green, metal doors. We were conversing, and I did not notice Dr. Dandridge had to use his key to open the doors. But when we went through the doors and he used his key to lock us in on the other side, I wondered where we had arrived. He turned to me in the most nonchalant, matter-of-fact manner and said, "Now, this is where you'll be working." I paused a moment as I looked at the desolate hallway with not even a sign of a nurses' station in sight. Still concerned about those green double doors, I turned to Dr. Dandridge and said, "You lock those doors?"

He replied casually, "Oh, yes, this is a locked ward, so these doors remain locked at all times."

Trying not to show my concern, I then asked, "So, we're all locked in here together, the staff and the patients?"

"Yes," he replied.

Just as he finished his reply, a woman exited one of the rooms. As she entered the hall, she looked at me and began to frown, as if she were angered by something. She was a tall, mature woman in her early fifties and was wearing a hat she had made from newspaper. There she stood, staring at me, when suddenly, in a deep, heavy, loud voice she said, "Give me a quarter!"

Her demeanor and her tone were so alarming that my response was to say nothing. I just stared back at her thinking, *Oh, my!*

Upset by my lack of response, she repeated her statement in a stronger, louder tone, as she took steps toward me. She repeated, "Give me a quarter, I said!"

I will never forget my first and only thought at that moment. After all my years of schooling, I could not think of one psychological theory, not one clinical technique for defusing the situation—nothing! The first and only thought that came to my mind as she continued to approach me was, *If she hits me, I am going to hit her back!* All my years of study had culminated in this one disappointing moment.

Dr. Dandridge, of course, was completely unfazed by the incident. In fact, he never stopped talking to me. He talked the entire time I was mapping out my combat strategy for the fight I was convinced was about to break out. As I was tensing up for the inevitable, Dr. Dandridge turned to the woman and said, "My, what a pretty hat you're wearing."

She paused, smiled, and replied, "That's why I'm wearing it!" She then turned and walked back into her room.

Just that quickly he had resolved a situation that could have made the evening news. I cannot tell you how disappointed I was with myself. I knew then that there was no sense trying to pretend. This job was not for me.

Instead, I took a position in the department of pediatrics, which had a special division that provided mental health services to children and teens during their hospital stay. This was a much better match for me.

But I was still left to grapple and speculate regarding why I had such an empathetic response to the patient at UCLA, but my only response to the woman in the psychiatric ward in the hood was to fight her. Of course, there is the fact that I was watching the woman at UCLA from a video screen. That was a significantly less threatening set of circumstances. Maybe, hypothetically speaking of course, if I had been face-to-face with the woman at UCLA and felt threatened by her, my response would have been to fight her, too. I guess we will never know.

However, in retrospect, I do believe that when I was face-to-face with the woman behind the green doors in the hood, old, familiar habits and mindsets arose from being in my very familiar context. I had reached for my very familiar arsenal of responses that had served me and protected me most of my life. Or at least, so I thought.

As I matured, I learned to use my voice and my choice more effectively, refined my "X," and found more socially acceptable ways for de-escalating situations. However, apparently the girl from the hood was still only a few layers beneath the surface, because when I felt backed into a corner, she showed up. And when she reached in that familiar arsenal, she pulled out what she felt was the best option she had.

Interestingly, while I only saw one option, which was to fight, Dr. Dandridge never got to the first step of feeling threatened. He reached for his familiar arsenal, just like I reached for mine. But his arsenal included a world of constructive possibilities. Actually, so did mine. That same constructive option that Dr. Dandridge chose is one that was available to me. To that extent, we were not so different. But for me, it did not matter whether the option existed, because, in that moment, when I needed it, I could not find it. All because of a difference in "perspective," which to some extent was influenced by his years of experience and my lack of it. It was clear to me that this was not the first hat made of newspaper Dr. Dandridge had complimented.

I am often confounded and yet comforted by the threads that connect us all. I realize that in the realm of human existence there are a finite number of human experiences. That means, to some extent, we are often replicating parts of each other's lives. What varies is magnitude, frequency, proximity, context, and the most potent variable of all—perspective.

The day arrived to begin my new internship. I remember taking my first walk down the pediatric corridor. Dr. Jamison was my supervisor. She was also someone I had worked with from time to time in research. She started our session with a tour of the pediatric ward.

I could not wait to work with the children. I was looking forward to seeing their little faces. It was not long into our tour when I realized this pediatric ward was not like any I had seen when I was growing up. We could not just walk onto the ward, because there was a security guard and a metal detector at the entrance. Once we passed the metal detectors and were allowed onto the ward, a delightful and playful young girl walked up to Dr. Jamison to greet her.

"Hi, Dr. Jamison," she said in a happy tone.

"Well, hello, Tamika, how are you today?" Dr. Jamison replied.

They continued to exchange greetings and a few jokes; then Tamika headed back to her room.

"What a sweet girl," I said to Dr. Jamison. "What is she in here for?"

Dr. Jamison answers "Oh, she has _______________," (a name I have tried for years to remember).

I asked, "What is that?"

Dr. Jamison replied, "That's a disease that comes from having multiple sex partners."

I looked back at Tamika as she was entering her room and thought, *But she's just a little girl.*

As Dr. Jamison continued the tour, we passed several rooms of children who had gunshot wounds. Dr. Jamison excused herself for a moment to speak with a colleague that was asking for a moment of her time. While she was in the hall with her colleague, I walked into a large room filled with beds. When I entered, I made eye contact with a teenage boy. I walked over to say hello, which triggered a wonderful conversation between the two of us. It was just lighthearted chatter. However, as we were concluding our conversation, he said, "When we try to go to programs that will help us or give us something to do because there's nothing to do in the community, they always shut down. We go back and the doors are closed."

I wanted so much to reply with all the reasons why he was wrong. Sadly, I stood silent, because I knew he was right. He wasn't just talking about programs. He was talking about programs that would be able to resonate with and make a difference in the life of a teenage boy like him. Glancing at the hall, I saw Dr. Jamison finishing her conversation, so I said my goodbyes to the teenage boy, whose words became an indelible part of my memory.

As I left his room, Dr. Jamison cautioned me about working with patients like him.

I asked, "Why do I need to be cautious?"

She replied, "He's a gang member, and the rival gang will sometimes try to come on the ward and retaliate, or they may even try to come after you if they feel you are associated with him."

We walked a little further down the hall to the neonatal unit. As I looked through the glass, I saw some of the most beautiful babies. Dr. Jamison informed me that some of the babies had mothers who had walked out of the hospital and left them. She also showed me an area where babies were suffering from the effects of being exposed to hardcore drugs in utero. Essentially, many of them had been born addicted.

Eventually, my tour ended, and Dr. Jamison walked me back to her office, where she introduced me to Angela, another intern. To help familiarize me with the ward, Dr. Jamison asked if I would accompany Angela in taking Autumn, an eight-year-old girl, to a testing session. Autumn was admitted for sexual abuse and had to complete a few clinical tests.

While we were walking, Autumn turned to Angela, who was a tall, curvy, very attractive woman and said, "I'll take your man from you!"

I could not believe my ears. I was looking at an eight-year-old child who was so confident in her sexual ability that she was bragging that she could seduce a man away from a full-grown woman. All I could do was hurt on the inside and maintain a professional game face on the outside. My mind was racing with as many thoughts as I had questions. Not questions that could be asked or answered by an individual—no, these were questions for the universe. All I saw when I looked at these children were different regrettable, condemnable, angering versions of "Y." They were the products of someone else's poor choices, neglect, abuse, and predatory behaviors. Ultimately, by some series of unfortunate events and adult failures, they were unprotected prey. I had seen enough for one day.

Well, apparently I was stronger than I realized. I came back the next day and stayed until the completion of my internship, almost a year later. My job was to provide individual counseling to the patients in need. I also conducted weekly group counseling sessions for all patients between the ages of eight and thirteen.

It was almost a year later, and the children were entering the room for my last group counseling session. I always started the sessions by making sure they understood that their participation was not mandatory, and they could leave the session at any time without consequence. I also informed them that there is no need to share personal information. Sometimes, they would share what brought them to the hospital. Oftentimes, that led us toward discussing problem-solving techniques. If their admittance was due to risky behaviors, my goal was to make sure those behaviors were not repeated. I would assist them in discovering skills, strategies, and motivations to replace their risky behaviors with healthy behaviors and maybe a little bit of hope.

This group session started like all the others. The children were saying their names, and those who wanted to were sharing the reasons why they were there. We came upon one teenage girl who said, "My name is Shawanda, and I'm here because I was sitting at the bus stop and a stray bullet hit me."

As the session continued and the children were sharing, my mind drifted. I began to think about all the devastation I had witnessed in the past year and the problem-solving strategies I had imparted. For one moment, I looked at Shawanda and questioned whether I really believed what I was promoting. Was it fair for me to ask these children to problem-solve, when clearly they were the victims of many of society's ailments? How do you problem-solve with someone who was just sitting at the bus stop? What did Shawanda do to deserve a bullet? Is it fair to even make them feel empowered over problems that even adults cannot seem to solve?

As the group paused for a break, I hurried down to Dr. Jamison's office and said, "I don't think I can do this anymore!"

She very patiently turned her chair toward me and asked me to take a seat as she quietly listened. After I had released all my thoughts and emotions, Dr. Jamison simply looked at me and said, "Michelle, we cannot afford to buy into being the victim. There must always be something we can do."

It was a simple statement, but for me it was a profound statement, because for a moment I had forgotten we were empowered. We are always in control of our "X," even in the face of a powerful, life-altering "Y." I had forgotten that even children are empowered with the ability to rise above their circumstances, if only in the smallest ways. It is our job to not only tell them they are empowered, but to also keep reminding them. Say it until they hear it in their hearts. Better than that, walk it out so consistently in your own life that it becomes a model from which they will examine, analyze, form opinions and maybe even immolate.

As for me, just that quickly, the woman who walked into Dr. Jamison's office downtrodden and in despair, walked out with a world of possibilities and hope again. As the children began to take their seats, I looked at Shawanda and said, "Isn't there another bus stop you can use?"

Our mind is a funny thing. It is so much more powerful than we often realize. Unfortunately, what we fail to recognize is often what we also are unprepared to effectively utilize in the moments that we need it. For a moment, the doctoral student had taken a step back and the girl from the inner-city, was front and center with Shawanda. Dr. Jamison did not give me answers which if I were honest, I was hoping she would and had a brief moment of disappointment when she didn't. But instead, knowingly or unknowingly, she did something more powerful. Her response caused me to remember that I was powerful, prepared, and equipped to find them on my own.

Indeed, when I look back on my childhood, it is not the hard times of the inner-city that I remember most. It is the voices of the Miss Jeans and Mrs. Thelmas that ring the loudest and define my memories. A true testament to the power of a voice, but even a greater testament to the power of a choice. I chose to focus on the voices of the warriors even in the midst of the most fervent competition that all of the unpleasantries of life presented around me.

When I asked Shawanda whether she was aware of another bus stop, I was in no way denying the fact that so many factors within Shawanda's environment were outside of her control. Instead, it was my way of moving the concept of hope and safety out of the hypothetical. As someone raised in the inner city, I understood very intimately how it feels to grow up with those two concepts, hope and safety, often feeling just outside of your reach. By asking Shawanda if there was another bus stop she could use, I was taking a moment and reminding Shawanda of how many factors were within her control. I was hoping that in the midst of Shawanda seeing so many walls limiting her choices, she would begin looking for and finding windows through which to view her possibilities.

My "Y" was Shawanda, and my way of impacting "Y" was to

remind her that she was empowered to search for and find new and viable pathways to take back her control. So, the "X" in this story is me, my choice, and how I chose to use my voice.

I remember that when I returned to the group and asked Shawanda about another bus stop, there was some initial laughter. But it was what happened after the laughter that caught my attention. Shawanda paused, began to think about it, then looked at me and smiled. That was the "Y" I was hoping for in this human equation. Shawanda understood that I was talking about more than a bus stop. I knew in that moment, which she later confirmed, that she got it! She understood that my question had little to do with bus stops and everything to do with recognizing and utilizing her empowerment. That was the goal.

As someone that has spent most of my adult life with "human observation" being part of my job description, I have found that oftentimes the hardest part of being empowered is *remembering* that you are.

Three:

Through a Child's Eyes

Few are the giants of the soul
who actually feel that the human
race is their family circle.

—Elizabeth Wray Taylor

Several years ago, I was funded to develop a prevention model for at-risk youth. After studying the statistics, I decided to focus on children placed in foster care. More specifically, I decided to focus on children in kinship foster care. Those are children living with caregivers who are relatives (i.e., aunts, uncles, grandparents, etc.). My attention was drawn to this population after discovering, at that time, that most kinship caregivers were lower-income elderly grandmothers. These grandmothers not only faced the challenges of parenting young children, but also many of them were parenting several grandchildren. Most of the children I saw them caring for were less than twelve years of age. The greater percentage of the children had some or all the signs and symptoms of being exposed to hardcore street drugs while still in their mother's womb. I often saw elderly grandmothers living on fixed incomes, running after toddlers and young children who frequently required more care and attention than the average child.

My response to what I witnessed was to develop an after-school program that used constructive play to: teach these children life skills; improve their emotional development; increase their academic performance; and provide respite for the grandmothers that were their caregivers. Some memories of the program bring a smile, and some bring tears. I still wonder who the program affected the most: the children or me? I think we all walked away changed.

Out of all the children that came through the program, two little boys (who I will refer to as Tyree and his younger brother Phillip) stand out in my memory. Tyree was streetwise and had a hard edge to his demeanor. The first thing that strikes you when you meet him is that he is tough and knowledgeable beyond his years. His younger brother Phillip was the exact opposite. He was a gentle soul who thought the sun rose and set with his big brother.

The first day of the program began with orientation. All the grandparents and the children were seated in a large open area of the building. They listened attentively as we explained the purpose of the program and all the amazing experiences we had planned. During the presentation, Tyree heard one of the instructors say the program was specifically designed for children in kinship foster care. Tyree did not know the meaning of "kinship," but he was very clear on the words "foster care" and did not want any part of it.

After orientation, all the children were escorted to what we called the "Activity Room." This is the room where they would begin a day of fun-filled learning and constructive play. As the other children were entering the Activity Room, Tyree, Phillip, and their grandmother were heading for the front door. On their way to the door, Tyree and Phillip's grandmother passed one of the staff members and whispered, "The boys don't want to attend because it's for foster children, and they don't want to think of themselves as being in foster care."

The assistant quickly ran to inform me of the grandmother's

statement, thinking that since I was the director, I would know exactly what to do. Although I was grateful for the vote of confidence, in that moment I felt highly overrated. I did not have a clue about what our next move should be. We had never experienced a child who did not want to be in the program. Having no time to waste, I rushed toward the front door to catch Tyree and Phillip before they left. As I approached them, I said in a slightly louder than normal tone, "Hi, my name is Dr. Jackson."

As Tyree reached for the door handle, they turned to see who was addressing them. Now I had to say something compelling enough to convince Tyree to release the handle and stay in the building. Having no time to come up with a better line, I said, "I just came to introduce myself and welcome you to the program."

Tyree quickly responded, "We don't want to be in the program."

As he answered, Tyree's demeanor and the interesting dynamic that was occurring between him and Phillip intrigued me. I knew I was looking at an eleven-year-old boy and his eight-year-old brother. However, when speaking with Tyree, I felt as though I were talking to a protective parent. Clearly, their grandmother had similar thoughts, because she never said a word. She just patiently stood to the side, as Tyree was the spokesperson for the family. It quickly became apparent that my conversation was not going to be with the grandmother. This was between Tyree and me. If they were going to stay, he was the one I would need to convince.

I immediately replied, "I understand, and thank you for coming. If I may, I'd like to tell you a little about the program in case you have any friends who might want to participate."

I proceeded to tell Tyree and Phillip about all the fun things we were able to do and that the program had only a few kids who were in foster care. Most of them were just staying for a while with a family member such as a grandmother or an aunt.

Tyree stood and listened. He never cracked a smile or laughed at my jokes. He was not going to serve as a barometer for how well my sales pitch was working. But Phillip was a different story. Although Phillip never said a word, his eyes and facial expressions said it all. As I was talking about all the fun and exciting activities the children would experience, Phillip's eyes grew as big as two moons. Shortly into my speech, his lower jaw dropped as if to say, "WOW!"

I concluded the conversation by telling the boys what a pleasure it was to meet them, and then I turned to walk away. As I was initiating a new conversation with a grandparent, I glanced at the front door from the corner of my eye. Tyree and Phillip were walking toward the Activity Room. An uncontrollable smile appeared on my face.

I watched Tyree and Phillip, day after day, as they settled into the program. It took Tyree a few weeks to acclimate to this new group of adults and kids. He was always careful not to reveal too much of himself or to show signs of having fun. But with time the positives of the environment won him over! Eventually, Tyree began to enjoy the program. Even more significantly, he began to enjoy the other children.

What Tyree was really enjoying was this wonderful experience called "childhood"—an experience he had completely overlooked in his effort to be a good parent to Phillip. It was as though Tyree had decided, or his experiences had taught him, that he could no longer count on the adults in his life, so he had to become one. It is unfortunate to say, but true: Tyree was a wonderful parent to Phillip. He always kept Phillip in eye's view and would check in with him throughout the program sessions. Tyree was always there to assist Phillip with his various projects and activities. He would even bring Phillip his lunch. I was overjoyed with how much love existed between the two of them. It was beautiful magic and sad all at the same time.

One day the instructors announced that the following week we would have a film producer visiting. The producer, who I will call Jay, was coming to help the children direct and star in their own short film.

The day arrived for the filming, and as Jay was setting up, I noticed a few kids teasing Tyree about his hair. The teasing did not seem to bother him in the least. Tyree was an African American boy with short, tightly curled hair. Typically, he would wear his hair natural, but this day he had put a significant amount of grease in his hair. It was so much grease that you could see some of it just sitting on top of his hair, as though the hair could not absorb any more of the product. As I watched him, almost every five minutes he would pull a brush from his back pocket and brush the top of his hair. He would brush one side of his hair to the left and the other side to the right, which formed a part in the middle. He tried to get the hair to lie down on each side, but when he would stop brushing, the hair would roll back up.

Shortly after he made his last attempt at working with his hair, he walked up to Jay and began speaking to him. Curious as to what Tyree was saying, I moved a little closer to hear but stayed far enough away so I would not appear to be listening.

I overheard Tyree saying, "I was wondering if you have any work I can do? I'm a hard worker, and if you'll just give me a chance, you won't be sorry. I'll do anything, even something real small."

As I listened, I was completely taken aback. The other kids were simply excited about making a film and were having a lot of fun chatting about it. However, Tyree was a thinker. More accurately, life had taught Tyree to be a survivor, and for him this was not playtime. He was trying to get a job.

When I saw Tyree talking to Jay, my heart warmed. Jay loves children and works well with them. I knew he would see the real Tyree and that their kindred spirits would connect.

What Tyree did not know was that Jay and I were good friends, and that I knew enough about Jay to know that he was Tyree as a grown-up. Jay's mother had been a drug addict. Jay told me about the time he finally looked at his mother and realized he could no longer depend on her for his well-being. He was thirteen years old.

As I continued to listen, Tyree offered Jay his charm, his wit, and a helpful hand. Tyree had truly presented his best self. Jay was cordial but gave Tyree little attention. He never even looked at Tyree or acknowledged the conversation. Jay kept working with the microphones and camera to set up for the shoot. Tyree walked away from Jay. He chose to sit alone away from the other children and appeared to be talking to himself in a rather animated manner. I wasn't sure whether the dialogue he was having with himself was healthy, so I walked toward him to assess what I was watching. As I approached, I realized Tyree was not talking to himself at all. He was practicing his lines. Actually, he was not just practicing his lines. Tyree had memorized the entire script. He was practicing everyone's lines and was saying them with feeling. When the cameras rolled, he gave his all, and, not surprisingly, he was wonderful!

I spoke to Jay after the program. We had a good conversation, but it was clear that Jay had not recognized Tyree's pain or his plea for help. Jay had just missed it! I had to pause to consider what I had witnessed. A man who has a tremendous heart for children and had wonderful insights, had connected with every other child in the program except the one who was just like him. I had to pause and consider what I had witnessed.

I later spoke with Jay about the entire incident. He was shocked to hear my account of the event. I shared with him my thoughts. I was waiting for a great debate to ensue, but instead, Jay calmly said, "I agree." I realized that for Jay, Tyree was living life as he and Jay both knew it. There was nothing alarming about Tyree's behavior, because it was no different from Jay's behavior then and now.

For those who may think this is a story about a little boy, you have missed the heart of the matter. This is a story about a child, a man, a woman, or even a man or woman who in an instant under the right circumstances can become a child all over again. This is a story about human survivors of all ages.

Tyree represents so many survivors walking among us. Some are adults now, and some are in the process of becoming adults. As I think of Jay and Tyree, I begin to wonder how much disappointment a child must experience before they lose faith in the adults around them. I think of how traumatic and devastating it must be to look at your parents, desperately need them, and be forced to accept the fact that they are emotionally unavailable. My saddest moments have come from listening to painful stories like these, realizing the unbelievable number of children and adults that have similar stories to share.

Do you ever heal from this kind of pain? I am sure you do but, "When?" and, "How long?" are good questions. Unfortunately, we will have to wait a little longer for the answers. After all, Jay was only in his thirties. Some moments of his life were wonderful. In other moments, a thought, sighting, or words from a passerby would, in an instant, take him back to age ten, still waiting for healing to come.

So often children grow up to be a product of what they felt forced to become. They are robbed of the opportunity to consistently feel wanted, safe, and loved and of the wonderment and beauty of what we refer to as "childhood." This is the most vicious form of robbery. Not only because what has been taken can never be given back, but also because there are few adequate substitutes to fill the void that neglect, abuse, abandonment, or even a general lack of time, love, and attention can cause.

Despite this fact, many will spend a lifetime searching for those substitutes. But those who prove to be survivors will eventually realize that the goal is not to rewrite history. Some men and women try to rewrite history by attempting to replace or recreate experiences they feel they were denied, or by outrunning the pain, filling their life with substitutes. The real goal for the survivor is to begin recognizing, in themselves, all the talents and attributes someone convinced you were never there. The goal is to realize that the people around you are only as powerful as you allow them to be. The goal is to now take control of your "X" and make the choice to love yourself enough not to make your past tragedies a life sentence. The key words here are "voice" and "choice." The question is: "What am I doing with mine?"

Restoration can come. The empty, wounded areas of your life can be restored, but you will not find restoration by continuing to rehearse your past. You must press through your past and choose to embrace and maybe even fight for today and for your tomorrows. You may have to fight hard when the battle is tough. You may have moments when what you are fighting feels relentless, but when you learn to fight affectively, you will not fight long. Victory comes! I created a quote that says, "Embrace your tomorrows and you may find your healing had been there waiting for you all the time."

As this story speaks to you, I hope you recognize your power to transform not only your life, but also the lives of others. Unfortunately, for me, this is a story of missed opportunities. Maybe writing about it has made it into a story of lessons learned. Jay missed the opportunity with Tyree. Maybe I was able to seize an opportunity by speaking with Jay.

Robert Schuller once said you can count the number of seeds in an apple, but only God can count the number of apples in a seed. I believe in the power of a seed. It excites and encourages me when I think about the fact that one seed can produce so much fruit. I do not know whether Jay was able to sow a seed in Tyree. Hopefully, I was able to sow a seed in Jay.

On second thought, why am I questioning whether I sowed a seed? That is the constant in our equation of life. The seed is one of the main mechanisms for impacting "Y." Some are good seeds that help us grow in amazingly wonderful ways. Other seeds are hurtful and generate damage that is hard to heal, and some destroy almost beyond repair. The most frustrating part of seed sowing is that, without your approval, someone can deposit a seed into your life that you never requested and that has no ability to do anything other than potentially destroy some of the most valued parts of your life (i.e., your confidence, your relationships, your motivation, etc.). The important aspect to remember is that although a seed can be sown without your permission, it cannot stay, grow, and form roots without your support.

There are also consequences for the seed-sower. In fact, you cannot sow a seed into someone else's life without that seed first touching your life. This is what makes both the equation and seed-sowing frustrating. It is the fact that they are both within our control and outside our control at the same time. The seed you intended for "Y" is also impacting "X" which is you. It is always there, always announcing who you are, and doing it with or without your permission. The equation keeps being an equation and doing what equations do, whether we like it or not. The same is true for the seed.

The fact is, we are always sowing seeds. Either we are sowing them in others, or we are sowing them within ourselves. The question I am attempting to pose, is not whether I had sown a seed in Jay. Of course, seeds were sown. My question is one of "type" and "quality." What type of seeds were sown, and did I sow good seeds? For me, those two questions are at the heart of the matter, because type and quality are what define my "X" and determine the ways I will impact "Y."

Don't struggle too hard trying to answer this question for yourself. Life will do the work for you. Through the principles and laws of nature, the answer is always revealed. It is revealed during what I refer to as "harvest time." What I love about harvest is that it is immune to spin and marketing campaigns. It's just pure, straightforward, and honest, with very little room for error in the answer it will yield. The tree will simply bear the fruit of the seed(s) that were sown. The entire world has an equal opportunity to examine, judge, criticize, or celebrate the fruit that will be produced from the seeds you and I have sown.

Four:

The Cost
of Changing
the World

Our lives begin to end the day
we become silent about things
that matter.

—Martin Luther King, Jr.

It was 2008 at a family fun day gathering. You could not have asked for a more perfect day. The sun was shining, the music was bumping, the smell of Caribbean food filled the air, while the sight of children laughing and playing at every ride and booth blended with the sounds and scents to create a wonderful, almost over-whelming, sense of family and community. Greetings and great conversations were sparking up everywhere at the event.

Among all the friendly greetings and good times, Jada Pinkett Smith stopped to say hello. She and I had shared cordial greetings before, so she knew I was on the planet, and, of course, I definitely knew she was on the planet. But this was the first time she stopped to chat.

We both were aware, albeit superficially, of each other's tend-ency to gravitate toward anything that might positively impact the world. Our conversation moved past casual chatter very quickly. That tends to happen when you have two passionate people talking about what they are very passionate about. The topic immediately moved to… what else—"making a difference." We talked about how sometimes it can be challenging to figure out the best ways to make a positive difference. How refreshing to be standing there talking to what felt like a kindred spirit about what felt like one of the most important topics to me.

I am not sure she would even remember the conversation. I am sure I will never forget it. We concluded by agreeing that even though succeeding at making a difference can be hard, it is important to keep trying. We promised each other we would keep trying.

Wait a minute! Let's back up! Correction: That is how we concluded *one part* of our conversation. Ultimately, the conversation ended because someone started blasting the song "Cupid Shuffle." Just that fast, all the etiquette and poise we had so beautifully displayed as we talked about changing the world was gone, with no evidence that it ever existed. For the briefest moment, Jada had what I call the "tennis match neck." She looked at me, then quickly looked at the people starting to dance, then back at me again, and as though there was no other earthly option, we both ran over to start dancing.

Actually, that is not true either. That's the second time I've been inaccurate in this story. The truth is, she ran, and when I say, "she ran," I mean like a "I'm not even trying to be cute or fake my excitement" kind of run. I, on the other hand, did a fast trot, which was a poor imitation of me trying to be cool in a moment when who cared anyway! My cool lasted for all of two seconds, and I took off running too. There we were, at least fifty of us, as happy as could be, going… to the right to the right… to the left to the left… It was good times for all!

Fast forward to 2018. A decade had passed. Somehow a video segment popped up in my social media feed. I do not know where the video came from or how it found my phone. Anyway, if I remember correctly, it was just Jada and her mother, and they were talking candidly. It seemed to be before any public announcement of an actual show. What they were discussing is vague to me. I just remember looking at the video and inside I knew she had landed somewhere very personal.

When I looked at Jada, her mom, and that red table, I said, "She's still at it!" I remember thinking, *she is still on her journey as I am still on mine.*

You hear people talk about *positively impacting the world* or *changing the world.* That statement can sound quite lofty and, to some degree, even arrogant in the assumption that you could be powerful enough to succeed. Speaking only for myself, the "world" is not the goal, it is the metaphor. A metaphor that has become the symbol of a deep desire to positively affect as many people as is within my ability to reach. Although I desire to see positive change, I understand that the word *positive* is defined by and subjected to my worldview. That means, like everyone, my definition of the word *positive* is inherently fraught with biases of all different types and tendencies. That also means, if any of my previously stated assumptions are even remotely accurate, then the notion of *me* changing the world becomes much more frightening than it is reassuring.

I do not have a definition for the word *positive* that will have the same meaning for you that it has for me except to communicate that we are both making the effort to put forth our own versions of being *constructive.* Second, at the risk of stating the obvious, I do not have answers. Neither do I have an interest in finding them. Therefore, the thought of me sharing answers with the world would be an illogical goal. My goal is to share discoveries that have the potential to support, direct, and on a good day advance others and myself in ways that make our life journey and impact on others sweeter and significantly less damaging. As a psychologist, I am constantly reminded of how much damage can and often does occur during our journey. Therefore, I am in pursuit of insights and information which reveal pathways that have proven not to be tumultuous.

My goal is not to *change the world*. My goal is to impact others in ways they too can define as *positive*. In other words, sharing discoveries is my version of the proverbial *change the world*.

Talking about "changing the world" causes me to think about a word that often appears in similar conversations. That word is *purpose*. I am not sure how I feel about that word. I guess it is not the word that troubles me, it is the way we define the word that I find concerning. Dictionaries and scholars so often define *purpose* as "the reason why you exist," or "an intended end."

I do not define my *purpose* as some ultimate life goal with everything rushing towards one primary life achievement. Sometimes when our search for purpose is focused on the future, we can miss the ways in which we are needed today. I believe purpose is fulfilled in moments, multiple moments. I also believe that a missed moment does not always present a second chance. I call these *purposeful moments*. These are moments when an opportunity to impact someone's life or fulfill something in your own life presents itself and there is a window of time to act. I believe that for most people, when they are desperately searching to find their purpose in life, they do not require an ultimate goal to achieve in the future. They are looking for what will give their life greater meaning and a sense of direction today and the next day, and the next day… Instinctively, we have a need to know that our existence matters. The way humans typically look for meaning in their life is by assessing the ways in which their life contributes to something or someone. In other words, in what ways do I add value?

Purposeful moments are meaningful thought-driven and action-driven opportunities that unfortunately are often missed due to our preoccupation with understanding the meaning of our life. Sometimes people confuse understanding the meaning of their life with living a meaningful life. There is a huge difference.

What I am saying about myself is that the thought of standing here today and committing to pursue an ultimate purpose that will guide my life for the next twenty years is disheartening. The only thing that comes close to assuming that position in my life is my faith. What makes me feel that my life is meaningful, and that my existence matters is my response to the purposeful moments that arrive in my life. I am adamant about not missing these time-sensitive opportunities to make a difference. The operative term is "time-sensitive."

Speaking of *time*, do you ever think about the fact that there are some things life only gives you a window of time to do/fulfill? One of those things is "skipping." It is not okay to skip as an adult. All the skipping you do not do by age twelve is lost in the sea of inappropriate adult, teenage, and young adult behaviors.

One day, many moons ago, in elementary school, my son Antonio came to me with a problem. He said, "Mom, my friend and I play in a sandbox the school has near my classes, and I know it is time for me to come out of the sandbox, but I am still enjoying the sandbox."

I replied, "Son, you will never have another time in life when it will be viewed as even semi-appropriate for you to play in the sandbox. Take this time to finish it. Play until you finish."

He thanked me and left. A week later he came to me and said, "Hey, Mom! You know the sandbox thing we talked about? I'm done!"

My son was experiencing this wonderful, rarely talked about thing called "resolve." Resolve is an action verb that takes a combination of courage and a dash of "I don't care what you think about what I have decided is right for me." Whatever being in the sandbox did for Antonio, he settled it. When he finished, the sandbox had nothing else to offer him. Both Antonio and the sandbox had done their work. It is funny how something as seemingly insignificant as a sandbox could suddenly have purpose for my son's growth and development. The purposeful moment I was careful not to miss was when he came to me seeking permission to finish. I understood that my answer did not dictate whether my son stayed or left the sandbox. Knowing my Antonio, if he wanted to play in the sand, he was going to find his way back into the sandbox. What my response did was enable him to further embrace his decision to remain in the sandbox and free him to enjoy the experience.

What is so wonderful about my son having the opportunity to *finish* is that finishing enabled him to peacefully move on to whatever was next in his life. The operative word here is "peacefully." That unbelievably rare, hard-to-acquire commodity is one of the unspoken, often overlooked by-products that is experienced as a result of achieving *resolve*. It is one of the biggest trophies in this whole marathon, although there are others. Even if "peace" is not your thing, and maybe you evaluate and identify life's trophies based upon monetary value and cost, the sandbox, or whatever your proverbial sandbox may be, is probably significantly cheaper than therapy twenty years later, which is simply designed to do the same thing the sandbox did—help you reach "resolve."

When you feel undaunted by the efforts of others to redefine or negatively define what brings satisfaction to you, that is "resolve." That is what Antonio found. My job was to respond to the purposeful moment that was presented when Antonio sought my advice. Antonio's job was to make choices that would enable him to achieve resolve and peacefully continue his journey with the benefit of knowing that the only thing the sandbox had left to offer him were wonderful memories.

I have looked at a few episodes of Jada's Facebook show. There I was, crying when Alicia Keys told the real story behind the song "Like You'll Never See Me Again." I was by myself, sitting on the edge of my bed, and rocking from side to side like I was at a concert, with everything except my arm in the air waving a lighter flame. I immediately downloaded that song onto my playlist. I am jam'n that right now as I write. There was another episode with Demi Moore and her daughters. Not only did Demi and her daughters have me glued to the screen watching, but then Jada and Willow had a moment together and… UGH! Tears again!

From time to time, I wonder what this show has cost Jada. No, I am not talking about her show budget for lighting, cameras, crew, etc. I mean the personal cost in tears, years, and everything life threw at her that she survived to get to today. Why didn't she just do a regular talk show and interview celebrities and other interesting people? Something as personal and in-depth as what I am seeing happen at the Red Table clearly comes with a cost.

If she only did interviews, it would be so much easier. In an interview, the person taking the greatest risk is the guest who is agreeing to be at least a little vulnerable as they answer questions and tell their story. But what I keep witnessing are not interviews. Instead, Jada keeps choosing to have conversations. Unlike interviews, in a conversation, both the guest(s) and the host share the risk. Of course, I am not complaining, because the viewers win. Conversations are so much richer than interviews. It is as though Jada took whatever risk that red table presented and pushed it aside. When she had every opportunity to design a show that skirts around her fears, tears, and vulnerabilities she just—didn't.

As I spew my thoughts across the pages in 2020, one of the most unusual years in my lifetime, there are so many new questions I am asking of myself and others. It feels as though so much of this year has been defined by what we never imagined. This is a purposeful moment that will become an indelible part of our history and pivotal in defining our steps forward as we also grapple with defining what forward looks like and feels like for a country and the world. It is one thing when a purposeful moment connects two individuals or a small group of people. But it is something completely different when a purposeful moment connects and or divides a nation(s). There is a weight, a heaviness that accompanies these moments as often they arrive bringing a bit of chaos before we reach the common ground, the compromise, or the full-on concession.

Hmmm! Chaos! This is another word that is defined by and subjected to our worldview. That means, like everyone, my definition of the word *chaos* is inherently fraught with biases of all different types and tendencies. One persons' chaos may be another person's long-awaited moment. However, despite all our many interpretations of the moment, we all probably can agree that the word *chaos* has a way of summoning our insecurities and revealing our strengths, or our lack thereof. These are defining moments in our life that not only call for us to look out, but to also look in as we grapple with the question that hovers over us all, "What will be my response to this moment?" In other words, "What am I doing with mine?"

I am not asking whether you would be willing to enter a sandbox. The question I am asking is, "Do you even know where your sandbox is, and do you know the pathway that will get you there should you decide you have an interest in stepping in?" The question of whether you would be willing to get in the sandbox comes much later. It only comes after you survive the journey that leads to the sandbox. The journey is the training ground where you build up just enough courage and a dash of "I don't care what you think about what I have decided is right for me" to get in and to finish once you arrive! There is no manual, so sometimes we stumble our way to our sandbox, our goals and to our truth, or to whatever we find to invest in that feels worth the cost. What I also have learned is that the path leading to the sandbox is seldom straight. It is fraught with dips, bends, and more than a few tight turns.

As I have rambled on, I hope you saw past the red table and realize that I am actually recognizing all who had an idea for how to make a difference, took a risk, and paid the cost. The list is long.

Whether we fail or succeed matters, but it is significantly less important than whether we try, take the risk, pay the cost, and enable our successes and failures to define our course forward and pave the way for those that might follow.

I smile as I am sitting and thinking. I smile because I find myself equally as excited about those who are not yet old enough to be outside once the streetlights come on. Too young to be outside past dusk dark and yet they are at home dreaming, thinking, and growing into symbols of strength and conviction, building their voices, preparing to speak, and maybe not so hypothetically.

I am doing a double pump up for all those great men and women I never had the privilege to meet but whose greatness I admire from a distance. Those who have chosen to share their pathways and discoveries and consequently have positively changed my world. The celebration should not be reserved for the ultimate destination. That is what funerals are about. The celebration is for the moment someone chooses to engage, takes the risk to try, and makes the first step regardless of whether they fail or succeed. Of course, they will fail and likely more than once. There is no other way to succeed. Expect failures. They are much easier to overcome when you understand that it is not personal; it is simply part of the journey for all of us. What others choose to do with your failures is part of their equation. It is a statement of how they are answering the question, "What am I doing with mine?"

Five:

The Power of a Gatekeeper and a Seed

Fear is not the opposite of success;
it's part of success.

—Ariana Huffington

There's something rather seductive yet inspirational about a sunny Sunday. It seems to almost seduce churchgoers right out of their beds and into sanctuaries everywhere.

I arrived at my church just prior to the start of service. The pews were filling fast, so I immediately began the hunt, stretching my neck and tilting my head upward to peer above the crowd, searching for a seat in my favorite spot. While searching I had the usual welcomed distractions from friends, acquaintances, and well-wishers poised with hugs, kind words, and general "how-do-you-do's."

This is what I call the "Sunday morning scurry." It can be a comedy show and a lesson in etiquette at the same time. The art is in being able to look calm and relaxed during the hunt. After all, parishioners would not want to appear competitive for something as insignificant as a "seat." But do not be deceived: For some Sunday morning regulars, the right seat can be the coveted trophy. Trust me, I have been asked on more than one occasion, and with the nicest voice and manner, "Could you scoot down?" As they are asking, I am looking around at the available seating in the sanctuary that did not require me to scoot.

Still engaged in light conversation and casual greetings, I finally arrived at my seat. After chatting for a while, I began to feel the stillness of someone from behind. I turned to see who it was. It was a familiar face, but I did not know her name. I smiled, said, "Good morning," and turned back around to continue my conversation. After a few minutes, I could feel that she was still standing behind me. I began to reposition my stance so she would be to my side, thinking she may want to participate in the conversation. As people left to take their seats and conversations subsided, she continued to stand there. Filled with curiosity, I waited until everyone left, then casually turned to face her so as not to appear rude. I sensed a friendly but purposeful tone in her voice as she introduced herself.

"My name is Francis, I'm so sorry, I didn't want to disturb you."

"Oh, that's okay," I replied. Feeling the need to rescue the conversation and fill the moment of awkward silence with idle chatter, I began, "...and how are you today... It's so pretty outside..."

Her eyes looked downward. Clearly, she did not hear one word of that insignificant dialogue I was apparently having with myself. Suddenly, she interrupted me and said, "You're a psychologist, right?"

I replied, "Yes I am."

She continued, "I wanted to talk to you, but I know this isn't a good time. It is just that my daughter... Well, I was wondering if you could talk with her? She's been having a little difficulty lately."

I quickly responded with my standard line, "I'm sorry, I don't do counseling anymore," and began to refer her to a local psychologist.

Realizing that we were only minutes away from the start of service, she interrupted me again to state her case more clearly. "I really want you to talk to my daughter. Camille, she has watched you and has a lot of respect for you. You might be able to get through to her and I don't know where else to turn."

I started to reiterate, "I'm sorry, I really don't..." I paused and was compelled by what appeared to me to be a combination of sincerity and desperation in her voice. I replied, "I am unable to counsel her, but I am willing to have a conversation with her and see if I can be helpful. Here is my number, have her call me." She thanked me and left.

A few days later her daughter called. We had a friendly yet focused conversation as she began to share her thoughts and concerns. Clearly, these issues were greater than what could be addressed in one conversation. My goal, of course, was not to try and provide solutions for Camille's challenges. Nor did I want to open more than I could close by the end of our conversation. My goal was to point her in what I deemed to be a healthy direction where she would hopefully find her own solutions. That felt within my ability to accomplish within our one conversation.

Camille was clearly a bright young woman with a world of possibilities in front of her that she simply seemed unable/unwilling to see at the time. I thought that maybe she just needed someone to encourage her, help her see the long game, inspire her by affirming her obvious gifts and intellect, and share with her both the struggles and rewards most individuals experience during the early years of adulthood so she would know she was not alone.

I began to share with her what I believed I was hearing her say, then I followed my plan. As I hung up the phone, I thought about how much I admired the fact that her mother was willing to look outside of herself and find a voice her daughter might listen to. Sometimes you are hoping for just the right outsider to walk up and say to your son, daughter, wife, husband, or friend the very same thing you have been saying to them, just so they can finally hear it for the first time. I thought that maybe that is what I was for her.

A few months passed. One day I saw the mother at church and stopped to greet her. "Hi, how are you?" I said.

She replied "Oh, fine." (Silence).

In the back of my mind I wondered why were we not, at a minimum, greeting one another with friendly how-do-you-do's? I took the lead by initiating the greeting. Afterward, I said a general, "So, how is Camille?" This was no more than someone would ask, "How are things?"

I noticed she was a bit slow to respond and appeared to be grasping for words that would answer my question but not share too much publicly, since, although no one was focused on us, other people were in the area. It was unusual to see so much effort being put into a general "How are things?"

Francis replied in a low but kind voice, "Your conversation really discouraged her."

Her response caught me off guard. Not in a million years did I expect her to answer with those words. In other words, not only did I not help her daughter improve, I did not even leave her in the condition she was in when she arrived. I made the situation worse.

Francis continued, "She said you discouraged her from finishing school or pursuing her goals."

I was speechless, and all I could do was apologize. I kept rehearsing the conversation in my mind. I do not sew, I am horrible at building houses, and you probably will never hire me to lay carpet, but my track record is rather substantial at counseling, coaching, and inspiring others.

I was certainly willing to accept that maybe somehow I failed in achieving my goal with Camille. What I had difficulty accepting was the message Camille took away from my time with her. After rehearsing my exchange with Camille in my head, I kept ending up with the same question: *How in the world did she walk away with that message from our conversation?* I began to think and reason with myself, trying to understand what happened. As I was sitting in church vacillating between listening to the sermon and thinking about Camille, my mind drifted onto the topic of my nephew, and I suddenly realized what went wrong. I had made the age-old mistake of relying on the language of words to communicate.

I am remembering my nephew when he was going through his teens. Periodically he would come to me to talk. Occasionally, in our conversations I would throw in an "I understand" statement, just so he would know that I was hearing him. Every time I would say, "I understand," he would get upset. He would say, "Stop saying you understand! You don't understand!" I would sit wondering what had just happened. I could not figure out why he would even come to me to talk about his issues if he did not think, at some level, I would be able to understand what he was sharing.

Finally, one day I just asked him, "Why do you get upset when I say I understand? What are you hearing when I say that?"

He said, "Auntie, you are making it seem like my experiences are just like your experiences, and they're not. I have my own unique experiences that I'm trying to get you to understand, and when you keep saying 'I understand,' it doesn't feel like you are really hearing me."

I realized that he meant something different and deeper than what he was saying, and I did not mean to say what he thought he heard from me. Confusing!

I have found that words often let me down when my goal is understanding. This experience also reminded me that when you are trying to understand someone else, sometimes patience and time can be your best friend. Some things are about process, and there are no shortcuts.

Second, I realized I was speaking "truth" to Camille as though "truth" was a universal concept. Of course, she did the same to me. Clearly, my "truth" was not hers. I now understand that even more than finishing college, Camille's true goal was happiness in all the peculiar ways she defined it. Most individuals would have listened to Camille and concluded that her process was concerning, which of course is why her mother came to me. But it was still the pathway Camille saw, chose, and was pursuing. When I suggested she reexamine that path, in her mind I was discouraging her from pursuing her goals, because the concepts were so intertwined. Next time I will try to hear more clearly.

So now you know my lesson learned and have some sense for Camille's journey. The problem with this story is that I walked away with a valuable lesson learned, but I was not the target. In the end you still have a young woman in pain, no clear perspective of how to resolve her conflict, and a loving mother still hurting for her daughter. When Camille goes through life and faces her next set of challenges, how many people, besides me, will search to find a lesson to learn?

I shared this story because there were a few points I discovered that are very powerful in unpacking my own equation. The first lesson I learned in this story is that sometimes both "X" and "Y" can have quite a "yuck" factor. Sometimes good intentions are just heartfelt missteps, all in the name of love, or caring, or general concern, or just trying to be a good citizen.

The process for solving the equations in our life is not always neat and straightforward. At times they can be a series of maundering moments, ranging from helplessly watching from the outside, to saying, "Here's a good idea I hope you use," to hoping that just the right stranger will come repeat what you just said so the person you are speaking to can hear for the first time what you have been repeating for the past year.

But the most profound takeaway that I received from this experience was the undeniable power of perception and the power of the gatekeepers in our lives to influence perception. How in the world could Camille have so many amazing qualities, look at herself, and overlook so much of her own value? Well, there are millions of average citizens, inmates, homeless individuals, wealthy tycoons, and others that could answer this question, because unfortunately it has become more of the rule than the exception. However, I do not need to ask anyone else. I can make it even easier and save time by just looking at my own life.

I have come to realize that life is less about what people say and more about what you hear and choose to listen to. I have been winning writing competitions since I was in middle school. I have written proposals for and won millions upon millions of dollars in grants, I have had articles published in journals around the world and scholarly reports in clearinghouses in Washington, D.C. Yet, I did not consider myself to be a writer. I was just someone that happened to be able to write. I did not know there was a difference until one day a friend and I were sitting in my dining room enjoying lunch together. She and I were casually conversing regarding our upcoming plans and a few thoughts regarding my desire to write a philosophical, biographical book of true stories. My friend must have picked up on something in my expression, tone, or posture.

She stopped our conversation, looked me squarely in the eyes, and said, "You do know you're a writer, right?"

That simple question was profound for me. In all my years, no one had ever told me I was a writer. I remember my pause before pensively answering, "No, I don't know, but I guess you're right..." I had no idea that saying the next four words out loud would change my life forever! After a moment to reflect and absorb her statement I said aloud, "I am a writer!"

Notice, in the sentence above I did not say, "I replied." I wrote, "I said aloud." I chose those words very carefully because I was so conscious of the fact that in that moment I was not talking to my friend; I was not answering her question. The words she spoke resonated with something that had lain dormant in me for too many years. In that moment, my response was almost instinctive, and I was talking to the whole world. It was not an answer, it was a statement. My version of a "Yes, ma'am, I am!" From that day, I have been confidently identifying myself as a psychologist and a writer. Those four words, "I am a writer," represented my version of the loudest exhale I could muster in the moment. This is the perfect example of why it is important to pick your friends carefully. They have access to the intimate places and spaces. What they sow in you can push you down or propel you to unbelievable heights.

One of my greatest passions is writing scripts—writing thrillers and action thrillers, to be exact. One day, my attorney at the time was at an event casually chatting with the head of a major studio. He began speaking about me. The studio head, who shall remain nameless, was interested, and directed my attorney to send my script directly to him.

I was surprised and excited when a few weeks later I received a personally dictated letter from the studio executive. I was so conscious of the fact that I was in the presence of a true gatekeeper. This man could single-handedly change my life forever! I literally tore open the envelope and began reading. The letter began with the traditional formalities. So, let me skip all of the "verbatims" and tell you that midway in the letter there was a shift, and this man told me in no uncertain terms how my ending ruined the script, how ridiculous my ending was, and how I would never be successful in Hollywood because of it.

I know you are wondering, "What ticked him off?" He was upset that at the end of the script, the African American character won. Actually, it was a team with mainly white characters and one black character with a few scenes that included his family. What my mother spent a lifetime teaching me about being able to achieve the dream, was overridden by this man within seconds. Something about his voice seemed more powerful than my mother's. I knew that my mother loved me, so her love felt like a "given." But the studio executive was someone that looked like a gatekeeper and had no allegiance to me at all. He did not care if it was me or the next person who entered the gate.

Regardless of whether they are the head of a major studio or a manager at the corner bakery, the characteristics of a gatekeeper are the same. They are individuals who understand the politics and the culture of the environments they control. They decide who gets in, who does not, who gets to stay, and who must go. The strength of the gatekeeper is not in the individual; it is in the individual's ability to control the variables and factors around them. That means, when dealing with a gatekeeper, it is not so much about "X" and "Y." The essential role of a gatekeeper is to control access by controlling the chain of variables we are referring to as "W" and "Z." These variables are of great value to the gatekeeper, because "W" and "Z" are correlating variables that can shift the balance of power.

We learn at an early age that the gatekeeper's perspective matters. We also learn the consequences of not staying in alignment with their perspective. The studio executive wasted no time ensuring that he clearly communicated and that I clearly understood I had violated his boundary. It is funny, because I never wrote a script where the African American was winning. I was writing the same script as Disney. I was writing a story in which truth and justice wins and the protagonist had a happy ending. As I said, perception is powerful, and perspective matters. I never saw the racial connotations, and he never saw my happy ending.

Sitting in my home office with the letter in my hand, now it was my turn to decide where to go next. I decided that no studio executive was going to spew his opinion all over a piece of paper, mail it to me, and I would simply absorb it like a sponge. I took that letter, filed it under "people who have issues," and kept writing. Oh yes, I kept writing. But as the years passed, it was only later that I noticed that I had stopped sharing my writing. I did not stay in touch with my "Hollywood Circle" anymore. I was still writing, but it was getting quite crowded under my mattress, because that is where everything I wrote ended up—including this book.

Do you remember in an earlier chapter I talked about seeds? Paraphrased, I said it is not a matter of whether you sow a seed in someone; we all sow seeds. It is a matter of type and quality. In other words, what kind of seeds are you sowing in others, and are they good, healthy seeds that will produce fruits that will be health and nourishment to our life or seeds that will take root and quietly poison our system? If for any reason that section of the book confused you, maybe this story regarding how this book ended up under my mattress will help make the point clearer, because this is what seed sowing looks like when you sow ill-fated seed in someone else's life.

Recently, I was vividly reminded of the potency and extended shelf life of those seeds. While searching through a few old documents the other day, I found a sheet of paper that had my writing on it. The writing was in red ink. It is not normal for me to write in red ink which tells me that I must have been compelled to write in a moment and simply grabbed the writing instrument that was closest to me and began documenting my thoughts. As I began reading the words on the page it appeared as though I was reading a page of writings in which I was talking to myself on paper.

I am known to grab a piece of paper and jot down a few notes in an effort not to lose a thought. However, these were not notes. This page of red writing was almost as if I had written a letter to myself. One full page of me talking out loud using paper as my medium for projecting my voice at least far enough to get my thoughts outside of me. But it was the words on the page that grabbed me.

This letter to myself articulated how I was feeling the moment I realized that it was becoming quite crowded under my mattress. Based upon the age of my children as mentioned in the letter, it was written a few years after my encounter with the studio executive. By this time, his reply to my script had been securely filed away in a drawer and untouched for years. But the red words written in my letter to myself revealed that even years later, his words were still informing my opinion of myself. However, the beauty of my letter to myself is that the words also seem to be a type of impetus for my turning point. The moment the seed began to lose its power.

I must be candid and acknowledge that as I sit here writing these words, I cannot believe a paper so relevant surfaced from decades ago just as I was publishing the book the letter is referencing. I would like to share it with you. I want you to read and experience the letter the same way I read and experienced it. Therefore, what you will read is raw and unedited. I apologize in advance for the poor punctuation and unpolished grammar.

One note for clarity. It appears at that time I had not formulated book chapter titles and simply had working titles. Therefore, I refer to two sections of the book: Precious Moments I and Precious Moments II. Here is what I wrote to myself:

Precious Moments II

I just finished reading the previous chapter, Precious Moments I. I am still reading these memoirs for myself with no concept of publishing them. It is 4 years later. Now, what was then my 7-month-old son has just started kindergarten and he is no longer just my son. He is my oldest son since he now has a 4-year-old brother. Why is it taking me so long to present it to a publisher? A book of writings I love so dearly and believe in so passionately. Some days I am confident this book has an audience. Other days I avidly question who it is. As a mother of a 4 and 5-year-old I find myself appreciative of so much more that my mother imparted to me. Precious Moments I is so real and so accurate, but it is far from being the whole story. As I re-ask myself the question, "What did my mother do right?" a plethora of examples come to mind all of which fall under 1 of _____ categories. 1) She guarded me (example: when men would say stand up and let me see how tall you're getting. That only happened one time as he studied my new blossoming into womanhood). 2) She allowed me to have a voice yet taught me respect. So, when I was asked to stand again, I felt empowered enough to say no in the politest but firm manner because she also taught me not to be afraid of adults. She raised me not to get a good job, but to reach my destiny and that it was ok to dream. Because you have to have a dream before you could make it come true. She understood how fragile yet critical the time is when you are formulating your self-concept and she protect[ed] my environment until such time when I could protect myself. She surrounded me with supporters/encouragers and made theirs the loudest voices. It is important to love and protect your children but at some point your children need to be able to love and protect themselves. Jamie Foxx said his grandmother gave him the tools.

Oh, how I love my mother's garden. She doesn't have a green thumb and is a complete failure at her attempts to grow anything eatable. But no one can beat her in cultivating potential, sowing into the lives of others. I realize now that there are all kinds of ways to have a garden. You can allow things to grow like weeds unattended. Attended or unattended, something will grow.

As I am typing the last word of the letter in this book, I am vacillating between feeling tearful and feeling embarrassed as I share this with you. At the point in which I was writing the letter I was not just a grown woman; I was a full-grown woman. I was accomplished. My clients were either Fortune 500 companies or names most of the country would recognize. When I showed up to a meeting, I was the juggernaut in the room. I was the executive people hired when the job was near impossible and they wanted the best chance of success.

Why would I, a full-grown clearly empowered woman, reach for that memory from childhood? The times, as a little girl, when grown men asked me to stand up so they could see how big I was getting. It is an observation from my past that I never think about. As I read the letter for what felt like the first time, I was taken aback by that recollection. I do not ever remember talking about that to anyone, except for a brief mention to my mother. It seems so irrelevant now that I am a strong soldier comfortable and capable on so many battlefields. But clearly, at the time that I was writing the letter, I was attempting to pull strength from a 12-year-old girl who, in the moment, appeared to be stronger than me.

I now realize that in my heart I was trying desperately to dig myself out of what felt like a deep well that I was hoping only existed in my head. I was trying desperately to take all the power and ability I would regularly summon on behalf of everyone else, and, for a moment, have it show up for me. I needed someone or something to remind me that I was empowered to create my own better day.

Back to the story, I was not upset that the studio executive did not like my story. That is just your typical "Hollywood" rejection. You expect that more often than not. You get the rejection, have an "Awww shucks" moment, and move on. What was penetrating, and what continued to take on a life of its own inside me was the fact that one of the most powerful men in Hollywood said no one would ever want my wares. That is what a seed looks like. A seed can be so subtle and powerful that it can penetrate the armor of the strongest soldier and live inside them undetected for years, forming roots that have the unearthly ability to invade the soul, define relationships, and impact destiny, and the strong soldier never see it.

But please understand, the seed is simply a byproduct of someone's "X." Seeds are powerful, but your "X" is more powerful, because a seed has no power, purpose, or place to grow until you provide the fertile ground needed for the planted seed to thrive.

Interestingly, something happened so recently I have not had a chance to share this with anyone. I guess it is a good time to think about it out loud with you.

So, I typically select the screensaver on my phone based upon what I want to constantly be reminded of. For the past few years, I had the same screensaver. It had a black background. On that black background was a lion, and in large, bold, white lettering were the words, "I'm coming for everything they said I couldn't have!" Every time I would pick up my phone it would remind me that I was on a mission.

My mother passed away October 3rd of 2018. For me, I didn't just lose my mother, I also lost my shopping buddy, best friend, the person to whom I told my best and worst jokes, the person that could look at me and see when the lioness was slightly losing her way and could say just the right words to get me to roar again… I lost a lot. When you lose someone like that, you do not allow anyone to tell you how to mourn or how long to mourn.

You do it in your own time and your own way, and you give yourself permission for mourning to take on a different form and presentation on any given day. My strategy for getting through the most emotionally painful time of my life was to let go of the past, wrap my arms around the future, strap on and pull forward all that my amazing mother had lovingly and methodically sown in me, and hold tight for the ride of my life. This was exactly what my mother would have prescribed.

I knew that the first step in breaking free from the past was to stand up and take control of what I had allowed a bad seed to do to me. It was time to clean out what was under my mattress. I did not have answers, nor did I have all the steps worked out in my head. That was okay for me, because even though I did not know where I was going, I was crystal clear on the only two directions I was willing to travel: forward or up. So, I went.

Fast forward. In rolls 2020. I'm going about my life, and I looked at my screensaver. For the first time in years, it did nothing for me. It did not energize me. It no longer spoke to where I was in my life. It just looked old and in need of being replaced. I had just finished a text message exchange with my friend Jessica. She commented that she had not seen my boys in a long time. I proceeded to send her a few pictures of them so she could see how much they have grown. One of the pictures I sent was of me and my boys just sitting on the edge of a fountain, smiling. It was totally unplanned. My son had parked the car, and we were out enjoying walking on our way to hang out at a coffeehouse. On our way we stopped to take a picture, which a kind stranger was nice enough to do. In the picture we are casual, not dressed in our best, my youngest son was in desperate need of a haircut, but I just kept looking at our faces. In my family, we do not pretend well. These were authentic smiles from a happy family. The picture was taken October 14th of 2019. It was almost exactly one year after my mom had passed away, and we were all right. I continued thinking about what saying or words of wisdom I should use for my next screensaver. Before I could give it much more thought, I had hit the button on my phone and the picture from October 14, 2019 had won the coveted position as my new screensaver.

Interestingly, I no longer felt the same compulsion to roar. You know, the most dangerous moment when you are in the company of a lion or lioness is not when they are roaring. The most dangerous moment is when they stop. I knew in that moment the lioness had arrived!

Six:

Pain So Undeserved

Safety and security don't just happen. They
are the result of collective consensus and
public investment. We owe our children, the
most vulnerable citizens in our society, a life
free of violence and fear.

—Nelson Mandela

I was just a little girl, but how well I remember the woman we will refer to as Mrs. Hillberg. She was a medium-tall, buxom-built woman known for being (and was commonly called) "The Mean Lady." Even if you never had a personal encounter with Mrs. Hillberg, her legacy was passed on from one generation of children to the next. You just knew to stay away from "that house." I think her reputation primarily came from the fact that she would not allow children in the neighborhood to retrieve their balls and other toys from her flowerbeds. What made this so difficult was the fact that her flowerbeds were planted on the parkway between the sidewalk and the street. Who knows how many race cars, Barbie dolls, and tennis balls were lost forever among those shrubs.

Mrs. Hillberg was a matured married woman, in her late fifties. She had one daughter that was grown with two children. Mrs. Hillberg's grandchildren would frequently spend the weekend at her house.

The other distinguishing feature about Mrs. Hillberg, besides the fact that she was mean, was the fact that she always kept foster children. I cannot remember a time when there were not foster children in her home, and always no fewer than three. Thinking back to those days, I realize that I misunderstood the concept of foster care. What I knew was that sometimes I would ask about one of the children that I may not have seen playing outside for a while, and I would be told, "They aren't here anymore." I just assumed that leaving was a good thing and that every child that left was placed with a wonderful family and lived happily ever after.

I did not spend a lot of time playing with the various children that would pass through Mrs. Hillberg's home. But Mrs. Hillberg's grandchildren (whom I will refer to as Robin and Jackie) and I would play together outside whenever they came over.

One day, Mrs. Hillberg's house was unusually quiet and no children were outside. It was strange to not at least hear murmuring of young voices. Curiosity must have gotten the best of me, because before I knew it, I was knocking on their door. Mrs. Hillberg opened the door as I braced myself for whatever she was getting ready to say in her typical stern manner. But, to my surprise, a slightly kinder, gentler Mrs. Hillberg answered the door. Afraid that her moment of kindness would be brief, I hurriedly asked, "Is Robin or Jackie here and can they come out and play?" Mrs. Hillberg informed me that neither Robin nor Jackie was there, and the other children could not come outside. Then, just as I was preparing for a quick exit, she surprised me for the second time. Mrs. Hillberg invited me inside to visit with the other children.

I remember this part as though it was yesterday. There I stood, looking up at her as she spoke to me from behind her screen door. I remember my thoughts and feelings in the moment. There was a little discomfort in knocking on the door, since that was something I normally would not do. I usually just waited for Robin or Jackie to come outside or they would wait for me to come outside.

There was an eeriness from the deafening silence at her house that was usually filled with the sound of children, the sound of adults, or the sound of both. Equally as odd and noticeable was her calm demeanor as she spoke to me. Reflecting back on the moment, what I was most proud of was the fact that I had no fear of the mean lady and she knew it. After an incident she and I had a few weeks prior, she never said anything more to me other than, "Hello," "Is your mama home?", or "Tell your mama to call me." I watched her holler at kids on a daily basis, but she never attempted to do the same with me.

A few weeks earlier, Robin and I had spent a lot of time playing together. Robin stayed at Mrs. Hillberg's house for a longer period than usual and Jackie did not accompany her this time, so Robin and I had all the playtime we could hold. The day after Robin returned home, Mrs. Hillberg spoke to me in a tone that felt a little too casual for my comfort. I have always been what my mother called "a nip-it-in-the-bud-person." I did not wait for ill-fate to happen. I would always begin eliminating the problem as soon as I saw it coming my way.

On this day I felt Mrs. Hillberg was getting a little too comfortable in how she spoke to me. To top it off, she called me "little girl"! I was always very respectful with adults as my mother had taught me to be. However, my mother never developed a tolerance for disrespect, and she never taught me to develop a tolerance for it either. I could understand her possibly calling me "little girl" if she did not know me or know my family. But Mrs. Hillberg watched my mother and father bring me home from the hospital when I was born. She knew my name was Michelle. In my mind, I had to nip this in the bud!

A few days prior to this incident, my mother gave Mrs. Hillberg one of my bikes for the kids to enjoy and have as their own. Since Mrs. Hillberg was pushing the bike into her backyard as she called me "little girl," I considered this to be the perfect opportunity to reminder her that I was not like any of the other little girls living in her house. I looked her up and down hard enough for her to notice and comment.

"What you look'n at little girl?" she said.

I answered, "My name is Michelle! And my mama didn't give you that bike. That's my bike. *I* gave you that bike!"

She was ready to blow a fuse. She started shaking and rattling the bike and said harshly, "Oh! Oh! You want this bike back? You want this bike back?"

In the calmest voice I could gather while looking her dead in the eyes, I said, "Yep! I want my bike back!"

She grabbed the bike by the seat and handlebars and tried to shove it at me so it would fall hard to the ground. I saw her scrambling trying to make that moment happen, so I was prepared. The bike went out of her hands and into my hands. As smoothly as it landed in my hands, that is how smoothly I began rolling the bike into my backyard.

She was furious and began angrily stating conditions on the transfer of goods. "Don't bring that bike over here, and don't…"

By that time, she was talking to a gate that was slowly closing as the back bicycle wheel cleared the opening.

It took a few weeks, but eventually calmer heads prevailed, and things went back to our version of normal.

As I stood outside the screen door contemplating Mrs. Hillberg's invitation, my normal response would have been, "No, thank you." But this time, I chose to accept her invitation. I wanted to honor this rare moment of civility she was displaying. But what I witnessed on the other side of that screen door made me never want to go back again.

Inside, all the children were sitting down watching television. As a treat, she gave each child a half stick of spearmint gum to chew. I do not remember all the children in the room at the time. My memory is rather vague on some details. But unfortunately, my memory remains indelibly crystal clear on the parts of the story I am sharing with you.

One child, in particular, is very prominent in my mind. We will call her Caitlin. Caitlin was such a sweet little girl. I do not know exactly how old she was, but I remember her being much younger than me. Maybe she was six years old when I was ten. A four-year difference in age is a big difference in elementary school. I remember looking at Caitlin and thinking she was kind of cute, but there was always something about her face that kept her from looking her best. There was always a puffiness and a weakness about her eyes as though she cried a lot or was punched in the face, but there were no bruises. I could not quite put my finger on it, but it was always something I noticed.

As I walked into the room with all the other children, Mrs. Hillberg offered me a seat to watch television. I wanted so much to go home, but I did not want to offend her, so I sat down. There was another adult in the room, and the two of them were sitting on the sofa engaged in conversation. Suddenly, Mrs. Hillberg turned from her lighthearted, jovial dialogue and began yelling in a strong voice, "Don't make me knock you in your mouth, little girl!"

Her statement was so sudden, and her voice was so strong. For just a brief moment I thought she might be talking to me, and it startled me. I turned to see to whom Mrs. Hillberg was speaking. She was looking at Caitlin. For the life of me, I could not figure out what Caitlin had done wrong. She was just sitting on a stool with her feet together, and her hands were folded in her lap.

Mrs. Hillberg continued yelling, "I will smash your face in if I see you chewing like that again. I've told you about chewing with your mouth closed."

I was completely confused. My mother always taught me to

chew gum with my mouth closed. But Caitlin was getting in trouble for that very behavior.

Mrs. Hillberg returned to her conversation with her visitor but changed the conversation to begin describing how she had disciplined Caitlin the last time she got in trouble. Continuing to laugh, Mrs. Hillberg explained how she had hung Caitlin by her thumbs from the avocado tree in the backyard. She then turned to Caitlin for her to verify the incident, and she did.

I could not believe what I was hearing. I remember feeling confused, because this terrible act was being discussed in such a lighthearted manner. She spoke as though it were the most ordinary behavior in the world. Sitting there, with my mind churning, I glanced at the backyard through the sliding glass door. Although the trunk of the tree was in Mrs. Hillberg's backyard, a large portion of the branches hung over our yard. Never would I have imagined that the avocado tree our family picked from and enjoyed had a little girl hanging from it on the other side.

Mrs. Hillberg then told Caitlin to walk over to her so she could demonstrate how she would grab a handful of the children's faces and begin smashing their faces in her hands to inflict pain. She included a few other demonstrations, still with a chuckle in her voice. I couldn't believe what I was watching. I looked at Caitlin's face, hoping to gain perspective regarding what I was witnessing. Caitlin just stood there like a little soldier, allowing these acts to be performed without the slightest appearance of a tear. It was almost as if Caitlin felt that her cooperation could somehow win Mrs. Hillberg's favor and maybe even some affection. As I continued to study Caitlin's expressions, it was almost as if Caitlin knew this didn't feel good or right but was trying to convince herself by saying to herself, "Maybe this is Mrs. Hillberg's way of showing that she loves me by correcting all the bad things about me that I never knew were there." Caitlin appeared to feel that if she could just learn and consistently demonstrate the valuable lessons Mrs.

Hillberg was trying to teach her then life would be good and pain-free.

Looking at Mrs. Hillberg as she continued enjoying her abuse, I realized that Caitlin could not be nice enough, quiet enough, or right enough to stop the abuse, because it was never about Caitlin. It was about what felt good to a sick lady who was so powerless in her own life that she had to make children her victims.

After a few years, Caitlin was sent to another home. As usual, Mrs. Hillberg immediately replaced her with another child. I could not figure out why the agency kept sending children to this terrible place. I am aware of so many wonderful stories of foster care and adoption, but when the circumstances are bad, they can almost be unbelievable.

Now, having the benefit of time and age, I realize that abusive adults abuse because of their own unresolved pain. I cannot think of anything more selfish than for someone to transfer adult pain onto the backs of innocent children—pain they never asked for, have not experienced enough life to understand, and do not deserve. Each time someone inflicts any kind of abuse on a child, whether physical or psychological, they are taking their own baggage, placing it on the backs of little children, and asking them to carry it. Unfortunately, most of these children will not only carry it but they will personalize it, internalize it, and be transformed by it. They will call it their own for decades before they ever get a hint that this baggage never belonged to them.

The second tragedy happens as these children grow up and spend many more years trying to figure out who to give the baggage back to. The problem with returning it is that the perpetrators seldom leave a forwarding address. In the realm of all that we do with our voice and choice, and ultimately with our "X," Mrs. Hillberg represents another end of the spectrum within our equation. I want us to be reminded and stay reminded that the other end of the spectrum exists. This is not a person that simply woke up, had a bad day, and a few other people had to experience consequences because of it. This is a person who woke up everyday understanding that their pleasure was dependent upon someone else's pain and proceeded to spend the day misusing their superpowers on the only individuals they felt powerful enough to hurt—children.

Caitlin, I hope you figured this out somewhere along your journey. I pray your path led you to brighter days. I hope life was eventually kind to you. I hope you find this book and read this story just so you will know you were someone so special, there was a little girl next door that never forgot you.

Seven:

When All Seems Lost

To do what you wanna do, to leave a
mark – in a way that you think is
important and lasting – that's a life
well lived.

—Laurene Powell Jobs

It was a beautiful day in October. The sun was shining and from my office I could see forever. It was October 26, my mother's birthday. The celebration was on my mind. When it came to my mother's birthday, every year was the "big one." Not because she was frail or had a pronounced limited number of days left to live. It was the big one because, in my mind, she was "big one worthy." I loved watching her surprise at all the different ways I would find to remind her of how much she is loved and how happy I was that she had been here for me to enjoy another year. Other than it being my mother's birthday, it was a most typical day.

Well, maybe there was one other detail that made the day special. A friend with a big heart found an abandoned dog on the street a few days prior. After posting flyers throughout the community and receiving no response, she called and asked if I would house the dog until she could find him a forever home. I responded with a resounding "yes." However, even without a first meeting, I knew he had just found his forever home. She dropped him off a few days prior and I was looking forward to returning home and enjoying our new family member – Kenji.

As I was preparing to step away from my desk, my cell phone rang. I sold my home and was leasing a townhome in the interim. When I looked at the caller ID on my phone, I saw the name of the leasing office for the community where I lived. It was unusual to see their name in my phone.

Then there was that momentary pause. You know the one, where you look at the ringing phone and ask yourself, "Why are they calling me?" Can someone tell me why we do that? All I needed to do was answer my phone and all my questions would have been resolved.

Back to the story. I did answer the phone. It was a staff person from the leasing office. She began by confirming it was me she was speaking to then proceeded, in the calmest voice, to tell me I would need to return home because my unit had a fire.

It does not matter how many times you have seen it in videos and on TV. Nothing prepares you to receive that phone call. When you do imagine getting that call, you definitely are not prepared for the person delivering the bad news to be calm as a cucumber. The contrast between what she was saying and the way she was saying it left me confused. Maybe I did not hear her correctly. I remember asking her to repeat what she said, "What did you say?" "Did you say fire?" She confirmed that she said fire. I cannot tell you why I was stuck on the calmness in her voice, but I was. I asked, "Are we talking about a small little fire or a real fire. She replied, "It was a real fire."

My mother was staying with me at the time, so my mind immediately went to her. Before I could get the words out of my mouth, the woman said, "Your mother is fine." I replied, "I'm on my way." I hung up the phone, grabbed my purse, informed my staff that I had an emergency at home, and left.

As I approached my unit, there stood my mother, outside in a housecoat and holding Kenji. Yes, indeed, it was a real fire. By the time I arrived the fire department had done their work and was gone. There was a man there that kept apologizing to me. I did not know who he was. My mother informed me he was the plumber the leasing office sent to my unit to repair my dryer. While repairing the dryer he cut into the wall to weld some copper piping. When he turned on his blowtorch there was a draft in the wall that carried the flames and created a fire he could not contain. That day, I walked away from the unit with my mother, our purses, our dog, and the clothes on our back. I was happy the children were at school. But they returned home to the same reality I was facing. Life had changed.

Management immediately transferred us into a corporate unit within the complex temporarily. If you are saying to yourself, "Well, she collected the insurance money, replaced what was lost and moved on," then you are mistaken. That is not how things occurred. The insurance money did not come immediately. After hiring a company to take inventory of all my lost items, the insurance company decided how much my lost items were worth. As you can imagine, the value was far less than what I paid. You learn very quickly that your $100 double-sided dupioni silk throw pillows in the eyes of the insurance company are just pillows. There is no box to check for fabric, customizations, etc. They are just pillows! If this were not enough, the property owner was so afraid I would sue him that he instructed every staff person at this large luxury resort community not to call me and not to respond if I called them. I made it clear in every way possible that all I wanted was for my life to get back to normal. I had no interest in suing anyone. Apparently, my message fell on deaf ears.

One day I received a call from a gentleman that said he was a plumber for the complex where I lived. He asked me to meet him at 7 pm at my residence where the fire occurred. I thought that was an interesting time for any of the maintenance staff to want to meet but I agreed. I arrived at the unit early. Shortly after, the plumber walked up with two other men wearing jeans and tee shirts like himself, but he did all the talking. He proceeded to tell me they could paint the unit, make the repairs and have our lives back to normal. I guess I was taking too long to accept his invitation so he then informed me that I should just accept what the owner is offering so I would not have any problems. He said the owner could make things rough for me.

He continued as I listened to him talk in detail about everything except the plumbing. Eventually, he realized that my silence was not passive. I was giving him enough time to say too much and I never stopped looking him in the eyes as he was speaking. I could see his posture shift as his initial arrogance was beginning to wane.

Finally, I interrupted him and asked, "And who are you?" He replied with a bit of head bobbing and hand gesturing that usually surfaces when someone is doing a poor job of lying. He answered, "I work for the owner."

"Oh, I see" I replied. I felt no need to talk. I did not call this meeting; he did. So, I was very comfortable allowing silence to dominate the room while still looking him in the eyes.

Apparently, he was not as comfortable with the silence. He proceeded to add to the offer. He informed me there are two other units the owner was willing to offer me. He said, "I can show them to you."

I replied, "Ok." We started walking to the other units. He described the interior of each unit as we stood looking at the locations from the outside. His two so-called "assistants" never said a word the entire time. "I'll get the key" he said.

By this time, I had seen and heard enough. This was clearly intended to be the owner's way of intimidating me while presenting his version of an ultimatum that made no sense because he was offering the only two options I was asking for anyway – to be relocated within the complex or to return to my previous unit after the repairs were completed.

At this point, these three men looked ridiculous. I was tired of playing, and they had picked the wrong person! I decided not to share what I really wanted to say and instead, I turned to the man and, in a sarcastic voice said, "Wow! You have a lot of information for a plumber and you have keys." I continued, "Let me stop you so we won't use any more of each other's time. For you to talk about paint for a unit that looks like that doesn't give me any confidence in any work you would do. Secondly, why I would be standing here talking about this to a plumber is a bit confusing, but I'll ignore that and cut this short. I have no intention of making any decisions out here in the dark with you and two guys. I'm not sure why the owner is complicating something that is so simple. Please inform the owner that if he wants to send me a message, he should put it in writing and send it during work hours."

I returned to the corporate unit and began recapping with my mother regarding what just happened. I'm sure I was a little too loud with a little too much animation as my mother chimed in on every neck roll.

When I finished my recap, my oldest son, who was only in elementary school at the time, walked up to me and asked a question he had never asked me before. He said, "Mom, are we going to be ok?" The power of his question was not in the words, it was in his eyes. I saw concern that only I should have been carrying. I decided in that moment, regardless of the delay in insurance money, it was time to leave.

I woke up the next day and began my hunt for another place to live. I felt so fortunate to have found an apartment my family loved. It was not far from our previous location, had a view of the city, was bigger, and had all the amenities that mattered to my boys. Their faces said it all and for me that meant everything!

I hurried and paid the requested deposit, fees, and advance

rent, and just that fast, it was ours! Suddenly, I remembered no moving van will be pulling up unloading our things. We didn't have any things! We needed everything from lamps, to beds, to forks. All we had was, what in a few hours would be, a big dark apartment in my name. So, off I went to buy mattresses, pillows, silverware, cups, plates, lamps, bedding for my room, bedding for each of the boy's rooms which they were excited to decorate in their own styles, bathroom towels, kitchen towels, a dining room table and chairs, a few more clothing items for the boys, hangers, and food to fill the refrigerator and pantry.

I knew we were okay when my oldest son came to me with the biggest smile on his face. While standing in our empty living room with bare walls, no television, and only a few toy options with which to play, he said, "Mom, we don't have anything, but it feels like we have everything!" So, our new journey began!

It was an unbelievable time. But when I think back, my mind never goes to the fire or the loss. What I seem unable to forget is the way some people made me feel. Those feelings became a catalyst in redefining so many of my relationships and definitely redefined my concept of "friend."

When the fire occurred, many people were concerned and asked if we were okay. I responded with my usual, "Yes, we are fine." But what stood out to me were the individuals within my circle of friends that, when I said I was fine, they simply moved on with the conversation as though everything was as it were.

One day I was having a conversation with an amazing woman who was new to my friend group which is rare given that I do not add to this intimate circle very often. We met a few years prior during a business meeting. One day she reached out to me by email.

Actually, let me clarify. She and I had a rare kindred connection at "hello." Our friendship was inevitable and welcomed when it arrived. One day during our conversation, that consisted of just girl talk, I mentioned the fire. My mention was so fleeting and was only included as part of a completely different story I was sharing. But, that fleeting mention halted every exciting topic we were discussing. All the fun girl talk was gone.

With a combination of silence and a somber voice she asked, "What do you need?" Trained to answer, "We're fine!" I replied, "We're fine!" I was fully expecting the usual response, "Okay, just let me know if you need anything."

I was totally unprepared for her response. She started thinking out loud and calling out a list of items she thought I might need her to purchase and send as she was in Ohio and I was in California. "What about a…" "Maybe you could use a…" The list went on.

Finally, she arrived at the last item on her list before she accepted my answer, "We're fine." She asked, "What about blankets?" "Do you have blankets?" I cannot tell you what was significant about the suggestion of "blankets," but for whatever reason, a decade later I do not seem to be able to forget it. I think it just seemed to be such a symbol of caring.

In that moment I realized I no longer wanted people in my life that trusted I would always be okay just because they feel I have always been okay. I wanted to surround myself with people who would ignore my short answer and begin making a long list of items I might need. I wanted to position myself to be in the company of people who would think of blankets.

Today, my friend choices are not only based on blankets; they also are guided by something someone said to me many years ago. I was having a casual conversation with a colleague who was from Africa. He was sharing with me about a woman he met. He was describing her looks, or at least how she looked from his point of view. His description was poetic as he described her skin color as the rich brown of cocoa. He continued and I was hanging on every word as he verbally painted the most amazing picture of this woman. When he finished, I asked him if he was planning to marry her.

He stopped, tilted his head as if there was a bit of oddness to my question and said, "I've known her long enough to know she is pretty. I have not known her long enough to know if she is beautiful." When he said the word "beautiful" he put his hand to his heart. This is the story that comes to my mind when I think of my friends. I have known all of them long enough to not only know they are beautiful, but I know how utterly beautiful they are.

I think the quest we are all on at some level is bigger than good times and great conversations, which are nice and have their place in our lives. However, I believe the bigger prize we are all searching for is meaning. To not only find meaning for ourselves, but to surround ourselves with friends that feel our life and well-being is important enough for it to mean something to them too.

Sometimes it feels like the world tries to convince us that "existing" is enough. I have spent a lifetime failing to espouse that notion. Existing is not enough for me. The quality of my life matters. My life matters, and the meaning of my existence matters. I am hopelessly and unapologetically driven by the belief that my life has purpose. I produced an Audible titled, "For I Am." In this Audible I mention being present on purpose. That is what my friends are for me. I pray that is what I am for them.

My friends make room for all my imperfections. In fact, their imperfections are a perfect fit for my imperfections. I love the fact that all my friends are adults, so I am not responsible for raising any of them and they never think of raising me. My friends and I send lots of celebratory text messages, usually about small innocuous moments that are profound to us. We wake up thinking about the fact that it may have been a few days, weeks, or even months since we last spoke, so we text an early morning affirmation or word of inspiration just to make sure the other has a great start to their day. We remind each other of all the ways we are wonderful simply by our nature.

I feel blessed to have some of the most phenomenal women and men in my life. They call me out when what I am saying does not make sense to them. I love that. You have to care enough to call someone out on their *stuff*. They are fearlessly optimistic about whatever we/they/I am pursuing. They never allow me to forget how powerful I am even in moments when it may be clearer to them than it is to me. They all bite when provoked. There is not a passive one in the bunch. My friends are strong, and their strength is complimented by their charm, class, wit, intellect, and compassion. Their strength is not ordinary. It is the strength of my ancestors.

I never think about it, but when it comes to friendship, I guess I too have a list. I know a few of the items on the list like integrity, trust, etc. But most of what is on my list I am probably unaware of and would struggle to find words to accurately communicate what is on the list. For now, I am comfortable knowing that it exists and is doing an amazing job guiding me. I pray that I am to my friends what they are to me. Not because I am keeping track. It is because I am always asking myself, "Michelle, what are you attracting?" I have learned that on your journey everyone does not get to go.

Eight:

The Significance of Play

Never underestimate the power of dreams and
the influence of the human spirit. We are all the
same in this notion: The potential for greatness
lives within each of us.

—Wilma Rudolph

I have a girlfriend I have known since I was three years old. Her name in this story will be Amy. What a special gift to have someone in your life to share a long history of wonderful memories and even a few moments for which we now have enough distance from the events to look back and laugh.

When we were young, Amy and I would play from sunup to sundown. We enjoyed each other so much and became disgruntled by anything that made us pause our play, even if it was a call from Mother Nature for a much-needed bathroom break. You could see us on any given day standing up doing the "Wiggle Dance," which was supposed to buy a few more minutes of playtime before our pre-bathroom grace period was up. I remember a few times our calculations were a little off.

There were so many things we loved to do together, so many things we dreamed of doing, and so many things we were precocious enough to actually fulfill. There were thought bubbles that never should have burst, but they did. We started a Girl

Scouts Club because I found my sister's old Cadet Handbook—we were seven years old. We wrote a book titled, *How to Become a Woman*—we were 8 years old. At the end of the day, like clockwork, you would find us racing from my driveway to hers, back and forth, trying to walk each other home as the streetlights came on. That was the signal that it was time for all the kids to come inside. But each time one person walked the other person home, there was one person that still needed to be walked home. It took a long time for us to figure that one out. Besides riding our bikes, skating, making mud pies, and catching ladybugs and little butterflies, one of our favorite things to do was hang out in my garage. You could find us there on any given day dressing up in my mom's old clothes.

But life in my neighborhood was volatile. One minute you are engaged in the most typical childhood activities, and the next minute you hear the clamor of something brewing. A husband and wife arguing a little too loud, hard, and long. As the intensity would escalate, you could hear the wife narrate and telegraph her thoughts and fears. "No! Don't do it…" There was an awkward silence as we called the police while waiting to learn whether our next act would be to exhale or to hear the unpleasant sounds of violence.

My mom housed frightened wives on several occasions. Sometimes they were in their nightgown or pajamas and with bedhead as they ran out of the house, with no time to care about how they looked. My mom was beautiful and classy, but she tolerated nothing from the streets and ran from nothing on the streets. That made our house a place of refuge in ways that most people never knew.

Or there would be the sound of someone fighting on the street. There's a specific rumbling and clamor that you hear just before the fight. You can hear the buildup to the outbreak. Those who are attempting to stop the fight are equally as loud as those preparing to fight. It is hard to explain if you haven't grown up hearing it. But there is a volume and tone to the voices that makes you brace up and listen. You either hear the person that wants to start the fight hollering every inciting statement they can think of that would compel their adversary to throw a punch, or you hear the loud pleading of a parent or relative trying to prevent what feels like the inevitable, or you hear a conscientious neighbor equally as loud trying to convince each participant to go back home. The situation is only exacerbated by the siblings standing by, ready to join the fight if needed. There you are with a big stew of individuals and emotions brewing, and all of it just crescendos in your ears to form one massive sound of danger. The feeling of danger is not because of the fight. It is because once the fight starts, there are no predictions on when it will end, how it will end, or how big it will get before it ends, as families will oftentimes come together to support their own.

But the fights, skirmishes, and arguments did not happen every day. The sun shone in our neighborhood just like any other. Families took pride in their homes, enjoyed cordial chats on the sidewalk while watering their lawns, and respected property lines. We lived every day with the potential threat that today could be one of those days. What I can attest to is that once any form of confrontation started, they would eventually end. When they ended, the neighborhood returned to our version of normal. You could find me and Amy riding our bikes, skating, making mud pies, and catching ladybugs and little butterflies.

One game that gave Amy and I the most enjoyment was called "Store." We did not play store often, because it was so much work. It took hours and hours to prepare. But when we finished… it was game on! For one day, my bedroom would be magically transformed into one of the finest stores Manhattan had to offer. We would spend hours drawing dresses, skirts, blouses, shoes, and purses onto plain white paper. After we finished drawing, we would proceed to color them with vibrant marker colors and cut out the items. We worked so hard and so diligently on each piece of merchandise. At the end of the day we would lay out everything in the room according to the type of item, and we would create departments: shoes, dresses, handbags, accessories, etc. Once everything was in place, the store was ready to open, and we were ready to greet our imaginary customers, who had been waiting all day for just this moment.

What I remember so distinctly about these wonderful, playful times is that when the store would open, Amy and I no longer really played together. We each had our own responsibilities in the store. Amy was always in charge of the paperwork, and I was always in charge of directing staff, helping customers, and managing the money. Once the store opened, she and I were literally in our own separate worlds somewhere near heaven. We would even become quite loud at times as our voices escalated with excitement. You would hear my mother or her mother in the living room saying, "Hey, you guys, hold it down a little."

Bottom line, Amy loved shuffling papers, and I loved being in charge. If you were to walk in on us, all you would hear was the sound of wrestling papers as Amy frantically moved them around from one meaningless pile to another. As the papers were being moved, Amy would use a crayon to put large scribbles on each piece. She would scribble fast with a flair as though she were a top professional at making those highly important scribble marks. These scribbles appeared to have great meaning to whatever filing system she was setting up. If you tried to ask her a question, she had absolutely no time to answer because of her commitment to moving her papers around.

It was the perfect relationship because I, of course, had very few questions. After all, I was in charge! At any given time, you could see me pointing to one of those paper outfits we had just finished drawing and cutting out, and I would say something like

"...and this is a lovely item that just arrived from Paris." These were genuinely good times and wonderful memories.

Sadly, Amy and her family moved out of the neighborhood during middle school. We tried to keep in touch, but after a while our lives simply parted ways. We were growing up and developing new friendships.

Many years later, Amy decided to visit the old neighborhood. In fact, it was twenty years later. She was driving down the street showing her two children where she grew up. When she arrived at our house, she decided to stop to see if anyone knew where I was living and how she might get in touch with me. As she walked up on that familiar porch and rang the same doorbell she rang twenty years ago, the door opened, and there stood my mother. Neither one of them could believe their eyes. My mother immediately swung the screen door open and invited Amy in for a wonderful time of reminiscing and catching up. After their rather lengthy conversation, my mother contacted me at my apartment, and Amy and I happily agreed to meet the next day for lunch.

The day could not arrive fast enough, as we were both filled with excitement. I pulled up to the house where she was staying while in town, and out walked Amy. It was so amazing to see little Amy as a full-grown woman. She looked the same, but everything was adult sized. I was happy that when I saw her, she still looked like little Amy. Time had been good to her. We embraced, exchanged compliments, and headed to lunch.

During lunch, I asked the question, "Amy, so what are you doing now?"

She replied, "I work as a secretary."

"Actually," she said, "I just changed assignments because my old boss wouldn't let me structure my own filing system. He wanted to keep a general system so that anyone assuming the position after me could transition into the position with ease."

She then proceeded to ask me the same question and I replied,

"I am completing my doctorate and my focus is on directing research." Suddenly, I was speechless and looked at her with a silent pause of amazement. I quickly said, "You are still shuffling papers and I am still trying to run something."

I could not believe that as adults we were still acting out the same behaviors we enjoyed in the imaginary store when we were children. Twenty years later, there we sat, two women in our thirties, still trying to fulfill our childhood wishes.

For many years, theorist have studied the concept and behaviors of play. A famous psychologist by the name of Eric Erikson comes closest to my view. He said, "play ... is the training ground for the experience of a leeway of imaginative choices within an existence governed and guided by roles and visions." But in my opinion, even Erikson failed to see the predictive nature of play as it provides a glimpse into how children define their contribution to the world and to themselves.

A few years after my reunion with Amy, I was asked to write the script for a public service announcement that would be spoken on screen by inner-city youth, and I wrote:

So, what is the significance of play?

The significance of play is that when I play,
I have the freedom to dream.

When I dream, I reach beyond the boundaries of
where I am to where I want to be.

When I extend my boundaries beyond where I am,
I raise my expectations for where I am going.

And my dreams are bigger than your drugs,
bigger than your foster homes,
bigger than your opinion of me, whatever it may be.

Yes, I am the hope of the future speaking out today,
asking you to think about the significance of play.

When I began writing this short script, I realized I was eight again, hypothetically speaking, of course. It is so vivid to me. I was not focused on writing for the project. I was intentionally using the project as an opportunity for my voice to be unleashed. A grown woman speaking out loud about seemingly childish things, and it felt so good!

It is true that every now and then we all go back to feeling eight years old again. Maybe yours is age six, or eleven, or fifteen. The point is, we all, from time to time, go back when we are trying desperately to resolve or achieve something that will enable us to move forward at peace. As a fully grown woman, Amy was still trying to find some place and someone that would allow her to unleash all her thoughts and ideas for how to process and organize systems involving paper. Without seeing her in action, I knew Amy was good at her job. I watched her as

she spoke. She still had the same passion that I saw in my bedroom when we played "store." As I listened to her, I was struck by how much had changed and yet stayed the same.

But I did not need to focus on Amy. I felt the same way about being in charge. I distinctly remember evaluating my success based upon how many people were above me telling me what to do. As a doctoral student, I remember thinking, *I have something to say, and I have ideas I want people to listen to.* At the time, I did not know what it was that I wanted to say or which ideas I wanted to share. I would tell myself, *When I get ready to speak, I don't want anyone to tell me that I am unqualified.* Yep! I was still trying to be in charge.

But what I was struggling to remain in charge of was me—my voice and my choice. Not only to have the opportunity to speak, but to speak and others feel compelled to listen. That is what felt so amazing when Amy and I played store. It was not that I had the opportunity to speak to every imaginary customer that entered.

What was utterly thrilling for me was that when I spoke, they would listen. I wish you could have seen their faces. They were engaged and happy as I directed them to everything in the store they were hoping for. I was young, but I recognized that emotion—happiness. The emotion that caught me by surprise was *gratitude*. I had experience feeling gratitude, but the store was the place where the person they were grateful for was me.

What felt so good about the little public service announcement that I wrote was the fact that it accurately captured what I believed then and now. So, what do I believe? I believe play is a powerful medium that to some degree reveals and fulfills our unmet desires. I believe when children experience the freedom to pretend, we allow them to practice the process of becoming. I believe childhood play and pretend are the places where great men and women experience their first vision of greatness. I believe the child in us never dies. It is sometimes deeply buried, almost beyond recognition. But the child in us never dies!

How often do we miss these valuable opportunities to peek into the windows of the soul? We miss them because we underestimate them. It is a time-sensitive opportunity both to teach and inspire a child. In case you think I am speaking exclusively about young children, let me be clear: I am speaking of children, wherever we may find them. That includes the child that, even as adults, still lives inside us.

Think about the comic characters in a superhero film. From the child's perspective there are only five types of characters: the hero, the villain, the person/people helping the hero, the person/people helping the villain, and the person/people who need to be saved or protected from harm. When you are in a child's universe, the question, "What am I doing with mine?" is actually asking, "What am I doing with my superpower?" As an adult, the answer to that question may feel complex and convoluted. In the mind of a child, even the child in us, it is quite simple.

In any given moment, the adults in our life occupy one of two roles. Either they represent someone to fear or someone to trust. Only maturity will allow us to gain enough perspective to see all the complexities in the middle or recognize the presence of all the other archetypes that make up the story.

I think we have all figured out that maturity is not proportional with age. So, there is no need to be afraid of acknowledging the child that lives in us. In fact, I hope you seize the wonderful opportunity to glimpse into and make discoveries in a child's world. I hope you become the vehicle to celebrate and incorporate those discoveries into every affirming moment you can find or create.

I believe a significant part of every person's greatness is encapsulated in his or her gifts and goals. Your gifts reveal your superpowers, and your goals tell the world how you intend to use them. I hope one of your goals as a member of the human race is to help set those superpowers free, both in yourself and in others. But only those who care enough, love enough, and are willing to sacrifice enough will have the insight and stamina to sow into the life of a child, or even into the life of another adult, the greatest gift of all. You ask, "What is the greatest gift?" It is to not only have their gifts and their greatness set free, but to have them set free in an environment where they can soar.

Nine:

Becoming a Player in the Game

Commitment separates those who live
their dreams from those who live their
lives regretting the opportunities they
have squandered.

—Bill Russell

This is a chapter many of you may want to skip. Go ahead, skip it. I promise not to be offended. Heck, I won't even know you did. Who wants to read a chapter filled with nothing but basketball. However, for those of you who dare to trudge through my sports analogies and can get beyond the thought of them being sports analogies, in this chapter you will find a few of the most powerful truths and insights I have ever learned, not about basketball, but about life.

The way in which the principles of sports parallels life is penetrating. For me and my family they have been life changing. On these pages are thoughts I have stored away for years. Actually, I have collected them. When something would come to my mind that I wanted to share with my sons, I would make a note of it in my phone. That is all this chapter is, basketball notes to my sons.

I am not convinced this chapter belongs in this book. I really had to give it some thought so I met with my executive board which consists of only me, spoke with my top consultant which is me again, and landed on an executive decision. I concluded two things: 1) I am never going to write a book about basketball so where else will I be able to put these thoughts; and 2) this is my voice and my choice speaking out loud about what is on my mind. So…welcome to my odd little chapter simply made up of a few, not all, of the notes I wrote to my sons about life and winning. My notes were about the game of basketball but with an understanding of their relevance for life.

Although I am sharing my personal notes, I am not including my interpretation of those notes. I will leave that role to you. Just a chapter of simple notes. That's what this is. Some of you will read this chapter and find great value as you connect the dots. Others may not find any benefit at all. Consider it a buffet. I hope you will take what you find most enticing, try a few new things that pique your interest, and leave the rest. Just remember, as you are reading my thoughts and anecdotes, don't spend so much time thinking about basketball that you forget I am talking about life.

Note #1

One day my son was at a high school basketball training session. They were conducting a one-on-one drill where one guy defends the basket and the opponent's job is to get past the defender and score. It is now my son Antonio's turn to defend the basket. The guy dribbles the ball up to Antonio and makes a nice move. Unfortunately, Antonio's defense was too strong for the guy to successfully finish. The coach looked at the guy and said, "Good move! That was a smart move. Now you need to go do the work necessary to pull off a move like that on a player like this. You want to play strong, but you haven't done the work to be strong! So, what you have right now is nothing more than a really great idea that you cannot deliver."

Note #2

It is easy to look at the launch pad and dream and it is easy to enjoy success. The hard part is everything in the middle. The seasoned player knows and relies on this fact to exploit every misstep and opportunity their opponent hands them. In the middle is where your first step becomes quicker than your opponents. In the middle is where you learn to see the court more clearly than your opponent. In the middle is where you garner the ability to create an illusion of movement and sell it well enough to make your opponent believe it and react in a way that gives you an advantage. In the middle is where you train, grow, lose, sit on the bench, learn how to come off the bench, get knocked down, get back up, and ultimately win. In time what you come to realize is that no one becomes magnificent at anything without hard work. Preparation is everything and the middle matters!

Note #3

The game is won by those who show up and those who finish. Keep in mind that showing up does not occur when you enter the building or when you announce, "I'm here!" You know you have shown up when your level of performance and contribution to the game compels everyone on the court to recognize that you have arrived and are a force that came ready to play.

Note #4

Information and ideas will only get you so far without the ability to execute. That is the problem with the dreamer. It's not only that the dreamer doesn't execute. The real problem is that the dreamer doesn't prepare and put in the work (the training) to be able to achieve.

Note #5

One thing about basketball, the closer you get to the basket, the tougher the game. The same is true for soccer, hockey, etc. The closer you get to the goal, the tougher the game. The reason the game gets tougher is because you have what someone else wants and values. In this instance, what they want is the ball and to deny you the opportunity to score in a game that has room for only one winner.

Note #6

You may know how to play basketball, but are you ready to respond to the speed of the game?

Note #7

What is the *pass*? The *pass* is opportunity that is moving in your direction. It is the moment you asked for the minute you stepped onto the court.

Note #8

All the bragging players do ahead of the game is irrelevant. The court is honest. In the game, the weakest link will always show up.

Note #9

All your skill is waiting for you to transition mentally and begin seeing yourself not just as a player in the game, but as a force that came to dominate.

Note #10

Get off your feet and go get the ball. You will never be aggressive enough to be great if you always wait for the ball to come to you.

Note #11

When you block a ball in an effort to prevent your opponent from scoring, you need to have the mentality of possessing the ball, not just stopping it. You can stop the ball and create an opportunity, or you can possess the ball and change who is controlling the game.

Note #12

You are not reading your opponents and seeing the mismatch. You are playing to the level of your opponent instead of playing to the level of your ability.

Ten:

Precious Moments

My children's eyes are fixed upon my life.
Their ears are tuned to my advice.
My every word they may not hear,
but I pray my steps have been loud and clear.

—Dr. Michelle R. Jackson-McCoy

I was sitting in my favorite chair watching my seven-month-old baby discover that empty plastic containers make wonderful bongos. As I was watching him, I was reminded of something I learned many years ago. I promised myself then that I would remember it when I had a baby.

Several years ago, I worked at a medical school as a researcher in the department of psychiatry. Once a month, the department would sponsor research symposiums and invite individuals from outside the university to come and share their research findings relating to various topics. As I was sitting in a meeting one day, the dean announced that a famous researcher, that we will call Dr. Juanita Casey, would be the speaker for the next symposium.

I could not believe my ears. I was going to have the opportunity to see Dr. Casey again. We met when I was an undergraduate. She had come to speak to our honors group, and I had been thoroughly fascinated with her research. After her presentation, the director of the honors program invited me to join him and Dr. Casey for lunch. I felt so honored and my "yes" came quickly. At lunch, we all had an opportunity to ponder new questions, share personal perspectives, and exchange fascinating ideas regarding the deeper implications of her research findings. What a wonderful and memorable time of sharing.

Well, it was five years later, and the day of the symposium had arrived. I marched enthusiastically down the hall to arrive early and get the best seat in the room. Twenty minutes later the symposium began, and in walked the dean and a woman I had never seen in my life. The woman took her seat on stage and the dean approached the microphone to provide the audience with a brief introduction regarding the day's speaker. I was still waiting for Dr. Casey to enter. I was thinking she might be running late. I became so preoccupied looking for her that I did not hear one word of the dean's introduction.

It was not until the lady sitting on stage got up, approached the microphone, and had begun her introductory words that I realized this was the wrong Dr. Juanita Casey. Not only was it the wrong Dr. Casey, but her research was of no interest to me. There I sat, facing her front and center with no appropriate way to walk out, doodle, daydream, or implement any other creative technique for combating the boredom. To this day, I do not recall anything about her research or her findings, but she told a story I promised myself I would never forget.

It was a typical morning in Dr. Casey's busy professional life. She woke up, bathed, dressed herself and her baby, and headed for the daycare center. They arrived at the daycare center, and, rushing as usual, Dr. Casey grabbed her daughter, took her inside, and said her typical goodbyes. While walking back to her car, she turned to glance at her daughter. Suddenly, Dr. Casey became overwhelmed by a very sobering thought: "I'm teaching my daughter how to take care of me when I get older." Dr. Casey realized she was teaching her that you pay someone to take care of your loved ones. What appeared to be such an insignificant part of their morning ritual suddenly became one of the most powerful learning experiences that would shape her daughter's concept of caregiving.

Personally, I feel that the power of the moment to define her daughter's concept of caregiving is dependent upon Dr. Casey's willingness and ability to create other meaningful, defining moments in their day. However, despite our few theoretical differences, there were some points that resonated with me in the most powerful ways.

That story taught me three things: 1) not to overlook teachable moments; 2) not to underestimate the power of incidental learning (unintentional or unplanned learning); and 3) to recognize how many teachable moments occur in a day.

There is so much that children learn outside the classroom that by the time they get to a classroom, a considerable amount of information and experiences have already informed their reality. As I was sitting writing and watching my toddler enjoy his homemade bongos, for just a moment I became frightened when I realized that I had a baby and almost forgot to remember what I said I would never forget. I am thinking of a few moments between my oldest son, Antonio, and I, which were similar in principle to Dr. Casey's experience. One occurred during my eighth week of motherhood.

Antonio and I had developed a wonderful ritual of staring into each other's eyes during his feedings. We would study every feature of each other's face. Our eyes would almost dance as they moved from one detail to the next. One day, while feeding him, the television was on and a documentary was beginning. I proceeded to look at the program while feeding him. Still holding the bottle and Antonio in my arms, I would glance back periodically to make sure he was getting enough milk and to check for spillage around his mouth. As I continued to look back and forth between my child and the television program, I suddenly realized that Antonio was no longer looking at me either. He had decided to study the furniture. Just that quickly, what was initially a beautiful time of bonding had been reduced to just a feeding session, and I was offended by the behavior I had taught him. I was teaching Antonio that feeding times had become about little more than just food consumption. Not that it's a bad lesson to teach. I'm not judging the lesson. I'm simply saying it was one that I had no intention of teaching him that day.

I wanted very much to be a good mother from both Antonio's perspective and mine. Most of all, I wanted Antonio's life learnings to be healthy and enriching. I began to think about my mother, Ruby A. Jackson. Don't forget the "A."; that was her favorite part of her name. Her parents didn't give her a middle name, so she made up one herself when she was a young girl, and she loved it! As mothers go, I always said mine was the best.

I am a mother now. It is my turn to successfully navigate this journey called "motherhood" with the hope that my son will make the same statements about me that I am saying about my mother. But what was her secret? My struggle to answer this question led me back to my childhood.

I remember always feeling wanted. What an undeniably profound way to grow up. Something so powerfully defining as feeling wanted. Yet, it can be so easily overlooked when it is a constant in your life. I am so grateful for my mother's life choices. I loved her "X." She never stopped enjoying being a mom. I am trying to remember a time when my mother was too busy for me. Not one memory comes to mind. That does not mean one doesn't exist. It simply means that if it does exist, it was such a rare moment and such an insignificant moment that it had little, if any, impression on me at all.

I remember Saturday mornings when I would wake up to the smell of bacon and the sound of my mother whistling beautiful melodies as she peeled potatoes at the kitchen sink. I remember walking into the kitchen, and she would already have pulled out my Easy-Bake Oven so we could cook together. I remember her sitting down at my tea parties pretending to enjoy the imaginary food. I remember the years when I had one short line in an hour-long children's program and how when I would finally step forward to say my line, I would find her smiling at me and still wearing her work clothes. I remember my mother and me sitting on the floor, going through old photos as she shared our family history. I remember she was always admired for her beauty and fashion. What most people never knew was that usually she also required cleverly hidden safety pins just to hold up those lovely secondhand outfits. However, as far back as I can remember I went to school known for being one of the best dressed kids on campus, and there were no safety pins in my clothes. She always saved the best for her children. I remember my mother's love. Oh, how I remember my mother's love.

As I continued to recall my childhood experiences, the answer I was seeking began to appear. What my mother understood was that relationships may be affected by major events, but they are built in ordinary moments. That is what my mother did right. She understood her "X," her power to choose what she would teach, in what direction she would guide, and how she would help define and redefine the world with me and my sister, Sheila.

She was a single mother raising two girls in the inner city, often working two jobs, and still bringing home less money than she needed. But what she understood was that despite her hardships, she still had the power to celebrate, and that is exactly what she did. She was thoughtful to enjoy, celebrate, and cherish the beauty within ordinary moments.

My mother also realized that her most precious memories, as a mother, would grow out of the most unassuming moments in time. Moments when you are simply going about the rituals of caregiving and you look at your baby and realize it is not quite "business as usual." Somewhere within the past five minutes your child experienced another unannounced growth spurt and moved to a different level of awareness, discovery, and intrigue. Their display of new behaviors will elicit either a positive response from you, a negative response from you, or a lack of response from you. But whatever your response, you better have some sense of what you want them to learn, because class is in session and you are the teacher.

My son Antonio, like most babies, studied my every move and from his observations would formulate intricate concepts and discover answers to complex questions such as: What does it mean to be affectionate? Are love and affection important in this household? Does it matter if we communicate regularly in this home? What are the boundaries? What facial expressions tell us when we have reached the boundary? The list goes on.

As a parent, keeping all of this in our consciousness can be a bit exhausting. Trying to find the balance can be equally exhausting. Little did I know that my answer to this juggling act of life lessons was on its way. My whole concept of parenting was getting ready to be kicked up ten notches and be changed forever, all because of one unassuming moment.

It all began with my best friend at the time, whom we will call Tommy. He had just passed away from AIDS. I still miss the laughter, life, and light he brought to me and so many others. I have always been someone that recognizes death is a reality of life. For the most part, I am accepting of that fact. But, my eyes still water from time to time when I think about Tommy. He was a gay man that loved God. No one could make me laugh like he could, and no one could make me get out of the house at a ridiculous hour like he could, to do something I would never dare to do on my own. And I cannot tell you how many lives he uplifted with just the right words, just the right perspective, and just the right scripture, at just the right time.

One of Tommy's greatest issues while he was alive was HIV/AIDS awareness in the church. One day we were sitting and talking about his wants and wishes. I could see in that moment my upbeat, high-spirited friend was feeling his mortality. I stopped him mid-sentence and said, "Tell me what you want to do and let's do it… and I don't want you to be afraid to dream."

He said: "Michelle, I've been in church all of my life, and I know these people are caring, but there is no one helping them understand this disease, because of the taboos around homosexuality. I want the church to understand that gay men and women are sitting in the pews. We are not on our way, we are there, we've been there, and we love God, too. We need awareness and education around the topic of HIV/AIDS."

Long story short, I wrote a proposal for him to receive his first pot of money from the church, then helped him receive his second pot of money from Los Angeles County. My amazing friend had a six-digit pot of money to fulfill his dream, and he spent every waking day of the remainder of his life doing just that.

When he died, he was replaced as director by a woman who was perfect for the job. She was a beautiful, early thirty-something heterosexual woman who had contracted AIDS. She was well-known nationally, was a friend to Tommy, and had dedicated her life to AIDS awareness. Unfortunately, shortly after assuming the position, she too passed away.

As a new mother and newly pregnant with my second child, I agreed to finish what my beautiful friend had begun. With a small but dedicated staff and the support of our pastor, we finished what Tommy had started.

The final thing I wanted to do as a gift and tribute to my friend was to produce a documentary film that moved those who suffer out from behind the label so all could see the human side of those afflicted. The film chronicled the journey of a young man that had contracted the AIDS virus. At the time, medical discoveries were lagging, and death was an all-too-common result of contracting the disease. The purpose of the film was to spark greater awareness, concern, and compassion within the faith community regarding HIV/AIDS.

The film featured a young man we will call Trey. Trey allowed us into almost every aspect of his life. Woven into the film were beautiful and powerful statements from celebrities and nationally recognized pastors. The film represented everyone coming together to say, "We must care, and they matter."

The film premiere was a beautiful event held at the Four Seasons in Beverly Hills. Keep in mind, it was the end of November. I was due to give birth the first week of January, and I was big as a house. I never imagined having to find an after-seven formal gown that far along in my pregnancy. Apparently, the fashion industry never imagined it either because there was no amount of money that was going to allow me to shop from the store racks. I went to store after store listening to personal shoppers find such eloquent, creative terms to describe what I looked like as they struggled to find positive features of the various outfits they had me try on. Statements like, "This one has a nice cascading flow that comes off of the midsection." I knew and they knew that I looked like what my Aunt Betty would call "a bunch of garbage."

Finally, I found a store that had a dress I fell in love with. It was beautiful! It was a classic, fitted, floor-length spaghetti strap dress. On the outside of the dress was a long-sleeved jacket made of stretchy illusion tulle for almost a completely nude effect, with a small train that trailed behind. The jacket was embellished with fine shimmering beading that formed an elegant lace-like print that appeared to float on the tulle. I had to have that dress! They only had it in a size 10.

Yes, the humongous pregnant woman bought the dress. I was

typically a size 4 and would be giving birth soon, so… All I needed to do was figure out how to get into it. I knew I would never be able to fit into the spaghetti strap dress by any stretch of my imagination. But all I had to do was get my arms into the jacket, and it could just hang open. I decided to go to my tailor and have her make me a long, fitted skirt and a spaghetti strap maternity top that came down over my belly. I bought a beautiful, smooth, taupe, double-sided satin.

Keep in mind that at this point, I did not have a cute little baby bump. No matter what establishment I entered, people would rush to help me, rush to take my money, and rush to get me out the door. No one wanted me to give birth in their place of business.

The night of the premiere arrived. I remember photos being taken of all the celebrities and influential people as they entered. Everything in eye's view was beautiful. As I entered, the camera man asked to take a picture. I remember smiling for the camera, and the camera man said, "Come on now, smile!" I remember being too big for the beautiful beaded jacket that was too small to even make it around to the sides of my body. It literally hung in the back of me like fly wings. I remember the doors to the ballroom opening and the murmur of the crowd. Everyone was passing compliments to one another and enjoying casual conversation as we entered.

I was enjoying a conversation with Angela Bassett when one of the pastors, who shall remain nameless, didn't just step on the train of my jacket—he walked up onto the train and stayed on it as I continued walking forward. I did a few low volume "Yikes!" as my shoulders were being pulled back from the tension on my jacket. Finally, he noticed and stepped off my train. He felt so bad when he realized what had happened. As he was preparing to give me a compliment that would hopefully mend the awkward moment, I turned toward him, big belly and all. He looked at my outfit and said, "Oh my…" (long awkward pause).

You know there's a problem when a pastor struggles for words. I stood there waiting for any type of compliment. I would have taken an obvious lie at this point. And what came out of his mouth? With a slight stutter, as though he was still struggling for words even as he spoke, he said, "That's a lot of dress."

But that night was not about me. It was about Trey. Before the event, the film crew gave Trey cash to go out and buy an outfit for the event. And my, my, he spent it well! He felt like a true celebrity and looked like a million dollars in what appeared to be a custom-made tuxedo. When he was introduced to the audience, the room filled with applause. Everyone was enthralled with the fact that the star of the documentary was sitting amongst them. Trey was so proud. Everyone gave him love, he felt the love, and he left with what no one could ever take from him, the memory of the day he made a difference.

Throughout the entire process my intent was to give to Tommy, even in his absence. But it is true that when you sow seed, some of the harvest comes back to you. Little did I know that a bit of harvest was heading in my direction.

The documentary we filmed was filled with well-known faces. One of those faces was Denzel Washington's wife Pauletta Washington. While filming the documentary, Pauletta arrived a little before her call time, so we had time to chat. Me being very pregnant, we started talking about motherhood and parenting. What struck me about Pauletta was how she would light up at the mention of her children. She has a smile and personality that can illuminate a room, and she wore that smile the entire time she spoke of her children.

In the course of our conversation I asked her, "Do you worry about your boys?"

She said, "Honestly, I don't."

The makeup chair was open, and it was Pauletta's turn. As we were winding down our conversation and my production assistant was calling Pauletta to escort her to the chair, I said, "What advice would you give me?"

She said, "Just be there."

I was almost not comforted by her calm, because I did not know how to interpret it. After all, most mothers use complaining about their kids as a bonding technique with other mothers. I was trained by other young mothers to worry about everything, then call everyone you know to let them know you are worried. So, I asked her, "Do you worry that it won't turn out okay?"

She said, "No, just do your part. Keep doing your part. It'll be okay."

Her advice was just too simple to work. I was listening, but it took a few more years of life lessons for me to hear what she was saying. When I finally understood what she was telling me, it was like a big smack on the back of my head.

Her statements did not come from feeling that she knew everything there was to know about her children and therefore did not fear that they would have a misstep. Her statements came from knowing what and who she had consistently been in the lives of her children. Who she had been was someone that spent their lifetime sowing into their lives. Her confidence came from the fact that she had trained her children for the inevitable misstep. Not that a misstep would not happen, but she was confident it would not take them out.

WOW! That flipped the script! I thought it was all about knowing your children. She just told me that it is more about knowing who and what you have poured into and have been in the life of your children.

As someone writing a book about "X's" and "Y's," voice and choice, it does not take much to figure out where my values are centered. When I reflect on that day, my thoughts go to two places. One, of course, is to the advice Pauletta gave. But the second place my thoughts go is to what she chose to give, because that is what defines her "X." With all the options she had in front of her, Pauletta chose to give me a response that was conscientious rather than common. Both options were available to her. Thank you, Pauletta, for seeing a moment and seizing a moment. Thank you for your conscientious "X."

Consequently, what I probably would have deemed as casual moments with my children before hearing her advice, became critical, life-changing moments after hearing her advice. They were moments I probably, might have, but hoped I would not have missed. Pauletta helped me see that although my children may have enjoyed whatever privilege was extended to them, the most important and powerful thing they were asking me to do was be there.

Pauletta, I got it. Amid making sure they had enough food, culture, travel, and playdates, your words helped me remember to make sure they also have enough of me. She was right when she said, "I'll be okay." I was okay. I am okay. My children are okay.

For me, this story was about being a mother, but at its core this is a story about who we are and what we are to the individuals in our life whom we love. It is about leaning in and showing up! It is amazing what can happen when we show up. It is even more amazing what it means to others when we show up.

I now realize our relationships, whether with children or adults, are either no more than what we make them or everything that we make them. I also realize that life is a classroom, and we must be very thoughtful of what we teach and what we allow our children and ourselves to learn. It is easy to send lasting messages that we never intend for someone to have. But, most of all, I learned to value and appreciate seemingly ordinary moments—they matter! It is in these moments when we teach and learn the greatest lessons.

Eleven:

Finding and Defining My Superpowers

There is no such thing as special
people. There are only ordinary
people doing special things.

—Unknown

It was girls' night out. My sister and I were at a café sipping tea, swapping stories of old boyfriends, and recalling hilariously embarrassing moments from days gone by. Neither one of us was able to complete a sentence before the other would interrupt with a story to top the one being told. At times, our laughter was so intense we found ourselves clutching our stomachs, gasping for air, and using every fiber in our being to keep from bursting out into a laugh that was sure to ruin the posh, sophisticated atmosphere of the café.

If you know anything about me and my sister, you will know that this café scene was an all-too-common occurrence. We are as different as night and day, except in all the ways that matter. We love each other deeply, support each other relentlessly, bring joy and laughter to one another habitually, and our "sister days" are a regular must-have!

As a little girl, I remember being so proud of Sheila. From forming a singing group and performing at the talent show in middle school, to watching Mr. Brown coach her water ballet team in high school, I was proud. My first plane ride was to visit my sister in college. She invited me to come spend the weekend with her.

Oh! Did I mention we have a nine-year age difference? Yes, I was ten years old hanging out with my sister in college. She fed me well, introduced me to more people than I knew existed on the planet, and took me to a crazy fun pool party on campus where, in my head, my new two-piece sailor bathing suit was the envy of all those college girls. I will never forget my thought as I was boarding the plane to return home. It was not about the fun or the awe of being on a college campus. My thought was of how my sister took such great care of me the entire time I was there. I was proud of her—again.

Fast forward to Sheila at thirty-three and me at twenty-four, and the age difference completely disappeared. We both enjoyed the same parties, the same makeup brands, wore the same color ("brown sugar") stockings that we grew up buying from the corner liquor store. In those days, people of color only had two choices in stockings: cinnamon/brown sugar or coffee. My sister's skin is lighter than my skin, but our legs were usually the same color, as she would stand next to me in her brown sugar sheer stockings feeling mighty fine! Both of us enjoyed checking out guys. She would work the big brother angle, and I was laser-focused on anyone that looked like a younger brother. Sheila and I grew up, got married, had kids, and the love affair between us continues.

So, as you can see, me and my sister in a restaurant, laughing until our sides hurt, is nothing novel. But this day at the café with my sister was getting ready to be memorable for all the wrong reasons. While laughing and talking about a guy we both knew, Sheila switched to a serious demeanor and said, "Did I ever tell you the guy was molesting his stepdaughter Rhonda?" When she told me, immediately I had an uncomfortable feeling deep in the bottom of my stomach. I was feeling the illusive yet unforgiving consequence of what I call, "ignored intuition," also known as "hindsight."

I had felt there was a strangeness between that guy (who shall remain nameless) and his daughter. I did not have proof; just a nagging, gut feeling I had never acknowledged. I was around them on only two occasions, but each time I thought the playfulness between them was too advanced for the girl's age. Rhonda also had adult responsibilities, such as cooking her father's meals. There was something uncomfortably familiar about their interaction, but I was not able to pinpoint the source of my discomfort until recently. This is the same discomfort I felt many years ago with Karen. Something about the relationship between Rhonda and her stepfather reminded me of my friend Karen.

Karen, pure of heart, was intelligent and outgoing, but a magnet for embarrassing situations. Many of Karen's days would have broken a weaker person. For me, her undeniable strength was part of her charm. I always hoped that people would see Karen the way I saw her.

Everyone thought I was so different from Karen. But to me, Karen and I were a lot alike. We had the same sense of humor, the same commitment to our studies, the same zest for life, and, most important, we had the same commitment to friendship. Karen knew how to be a good friend. It was always important to me that I be as good of a friend to her as she was to me. I hope I lived up to that. I have not seen Karen for quite some time. However, even to this day, a thought back to one of our jokes can make me laugh, and the good times we shared still put a smile on my face.

Karen and I had been friends for several years when one day I noticed something about Karen felt different. I asked her if she was okay. She shared with me that her father had molested her for most of her life. I was completely shocked. I tried to keep a calm face to comfort her, but inside I was thinking, *But your house is so nice, and you dress so nice, and your parents both have good jobs, and...* As if those things really mattered.

Karen said, "One day he just stopped coming into my room, and I never knew why, until last night when we caught him in the kitchen with my little sister."

At this point I was floored but also humbled by Karen's strength. I said, "Do you think you were able to stop him before he could do anything to her?"

She looked down with solemn eyes and said, "She had stains on her nightgown, and he was on his knees with his pants unzipped and open."

When Karen told me, I was admittedly outraged but also it explained so many things. Karen had always sought the approval of her father, and he had always left her wanting it. She had lots of adult responsibilities, as though she was his wife. She was responsible for having her father's dinner ready when he came home, because her mother's job required her to work late into the night. Shortly after Karen's father was caught, he left the family. He left Karen and her little sister to heal in whatever way they could, without the slightest sign of remorse from him.

My thoughts left Karen and returned to the unfortunate conversation I was having with my sister. I proceeded to ask her, "What did you do when Rhonda told you she was being sexually abused?"

My sister replied with the only unacceptable answer: "Nothing..."

I looked at her with shock in my eyes as I interrupted her. "How could a young girl share that kind of information with you and you do nothing? Don't you realize she wasn't telling you just to share the information, she was crying out for help—and you did nothing!"

My sister proceeded to finish the sentence I interrupted. She told me the various ways she attempted to intervene. She said unfortunately there was not much she could do, because Rhonda's mother was ignoring the problem and chose not to believe Rhonda was telling the truth. Eventually, Rhonda's mother asked my sister to "mind her own business." I was so proud that my sister made a valiant effort. I was proud that she led with her heart and her conviction. But in that moment, I was saddened, because I am a firm believer that there is always something we can do. In fact, there must always be something we can do.

As I sit professing my beliefs, I am reminded of my own encounters with children who were either victimized, traumatized, or hurting in one way or another. It was my first apartment. After living there for approximately two years, a man and young boy moved into the apartment right across from my front window. I had such an uncomfortable feeling about their relationship. I could not put my finger on it, but there was an oddness about it. The little boy was about four years old, and the man never let him out to play. They always had the drapes pulled, and the only time they would come out of the apartment was to go to the car. Upon their return, they would quickly go back into the apartment.

The little boy did not have the relaxed nature that you find among children. When they would walk to the car the man always held the boy's hand, kept him close and seemed uncomfortable with any kind of friendly conversation with the neighbors.

In my gut, I truly felt this was a father that had stolen his son from the mother, and somewhere out there was a mother wondering where her child was and if he was okay. My worst fear was the thought that this man might not be the boy's father and was instead a predator. That also meant this was possibly a little boy wondering why his mother or father had not come to rescue him. More relevant for me was the possibility that he was wondering why the adults that were passing him every day were unable to or did not care enough to make a difference.

Finally, I became so uncomfortable with the peculiarities of their relationship that I called the Department of Children and Family Services to have a social worker come out and at least check into the situation. To my dismay, that call ended almost as quickly as it began. They initiated the conversation by asking me what evidence I had that there may be abuse occurring in the home. Clearly, what I had to share was far from what they would consider "evidence." A few months later, I moved out of the apartment. I never forgot the little boy. He remained in my prayers for years.

Another encounter occurred while I was driving down the street one day. I stopped at a red light next to an old, beat-up, light blue, Chevy truck. Sitting in the truck was a matured Caucasian man. He looked as though he may have been in his late sixties, but his face was quite weathered and wrinkled for his years. The fact that he had no teeth added to his aged look. Sitting next to him in the truck was the cutest little curly haired biracial boy. The front seat of the truck went all the way across, so the boy was literally sitting in the middle of the seat, right next to the man. The young boy looked to be approximately five or six years of age.

As I pulled up to the stoplight, I noticed the man looking at me. In order not to be rude, I turned my head slightly to give a very casual but friendly smile. When I smiled, he immediately proceeded to lean out his window and simulate oral sex with his mouth. It caught me so off guard with what felt like a never-ending display of explicit, toothless mouth gyrations. It was one of the most pathetic sights I had ever seen, and all of it had transpired in front of the boy.

Hoping that my lack of response would cause him to cease, I immediately turned away without acknowledging the shock value of his behavior. Unfortunately, ignoring him did not affect his behavior in the least. As I continued driving, picking up speed to remove myself from his direct view, he stayed side-by-side with my car, performing his lewd acts while driving and hanging out the window. I drove faster, and he drove faster. I slowed down, and he slowed down. The man then began to shout profanities out the window that inferred what he wanted to do to me sexually. He used the most vulgar, explicit language possible. Eventually, I was able to make a quick left turn and lose him.

From time to time I think back to that incident. Interestingly, my thoughts never go to the man; my thoughts consistently go to the boy sitting by his side. The lack of apprehension this man displayed was alarming to me, to say the least. I was haunted by the man's complete disregard for the potential impact of his lewd acts on such a young, impressionable mind, which, for me, was unconscionable. I can only imagine what that little boy must have seen and maybe experienced in his short lifetime.

I realize that some people might read this story and conclude that I just have a vivid imagination. Maybe these children were not in danger at all. They may be correct, but the risk that they could be wrong is more risk than I can ever be comfortable taking.

The first casualties may have been Karen and Rhonda, but the other casualty was me, when I felt powerless because someone told me what could not be done, and I believed them. The casualty did not occur when they told me nothing could be done. The casualty occurred when I believed them. The issue turns on the question, "How much do you care?" You see, I cared about the little boy in the apartment; otherwise, what I saw would not have disturbed me, and I never would have made the call. But did I care enough? I did not care enough that when the system appeared to push me in a corner I would rise and push back. The world is full of caring people, but do we care enough to make a difference that can be felt by the person(s) in need of help?

We hear about so many casualties, that it is easy to become immune to the sound of tragedy. But the unfortunate by-product of becoming immune to tragedy is that our ears will still hear the laughter but will become deaf to the cry for help. This is a story of the painful "Y's." When "Y" hurts and the voice and choice of those positioned to be heroes feels silenced and ineffective. When only the ones that hurt you feel powerful. When there appears to be no superpower on the side of good, and your heroes seem too hard to find.

In the stories we grew up watching and reading there was always someone that would eventually rescue you. The victim just had to survive long enough for the hero to arrive and save them. But what a horrible feeling to have to realize that no one is coming. As you think about your own life, I hope this story will help remind you that the feeling of helplessness and hopelessness is not bound by age. This is exactly how you become eight again, six again, fifteen again. We go back to the places where we felt power-less.

I can hear someone saying, "That's obvious, we know help-lessness and hopelessness is not bound by age." But I am not asking you to know it with your head; I am asking you to see it and feel it with your heart. I am asking for situations to matter enough for you not to just read and judge my stories, but to take a look at your own stories, even the one you are writing right now by your voice and choice as you read my stories.

The other point I have learned, and it is so important for me to say out loud, is that I get to choose how I make a difference on the planet. Yes, I am fully in charge of my "X." It is an odd thing, that once you show the world you have a great capacity to care, there will always be people who will have their own interpretation of how that should manifest. Their interpretation is often followed by a proposition for something they feel very strongly that you should do. Along with their propositions and interpretations will also come little space for you to comfortably say "no" to whatever they are hoping you will do. There will be guilt feelings you will fight as others so graciously disseminate moral propositions everywhere except in their own backyard.

Sometimes it is hard to say "no" and feel good about it. I have found that your best "no's" come in times when the "yes" others are looking for is not yours to give. It is most likely a "yes" that belongs squarely on their shoulders that they are working to place on yours. In those moments, remember what you probably learned in kindergarten: "Don't take what doesn't belong to you!"

Yes, the rumors are true. It is a proven fact. Research has thoroughly shown you cannot be all things to all people. So, be careful about allowing outside voices to become louder in your ear than your own voice. Just remember, the word "no" is a viable answer that does not require an explanation. The ability to decide when and if to say "yes" or "no" is one of the great privileges of having a voice and a choice.

This book represents one way that I am showing up, and not hypothetically. What I have discovered is that when I am solving for "X" and care about "Y," it often requires a little sacrifice, a little risk taking, and a lot of turning my evaluation and judgment from looking at you to looking at me and how I am responding to the world around me. To ask and answer the question which, by now you should know where I am going with this… The question is, "What am I doing with mine?" This question is not an opportunity to make a list of all the ways celebrities and politicians can make a difference. Your list is exclusively for you. What is in your realm of influence? In what ways can you wake up and make a tangible difference that you or someone else can feel? The key to becoming part of any solution is in not thinking, "Change the world." Instead, it would be wonderful if we could all agree on the importance of at least intentionally touching it. That would be an amazing start.

What I hope you have discovered in this chapter is "your part" and understanding that it is okay for your "X" to be a work in progress; all of them are.

Twelve:

You Put Me in What Category?

When people tell you all the reasons
why things can't be done, remember all
the times they've been wrong.

—Unknown

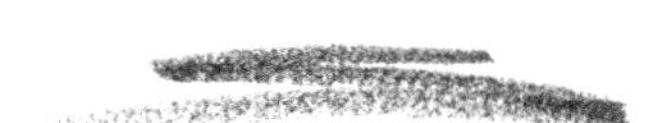

It was my first year of college. I recall sitting in the student union. My books were open, but my mind had drifted, and I had long since drowned out the murmurs of conversations that surrounded me. I was sitting there trying to figure out where I could find a part-time job that would fit around the scattered class schedule I had that semester. No bright ideas were coming to mind, so I decided to walk around campus to kill time before my next class.

My steps took me to the career center job board. As I scanned the board, I noticed a lot of parents were requesting tutoring for their children. Something immediately clicked in my head, and I had my answer. I would open my own tutorial service. I wrote down the names and contact information of a couple of parents inquiring regarding tutoring in math and proceeded to call them. I selected clients in the affluent areas so they would be able to afford my exorbitant price of ten dollars per hour. I also offered free tutoring twice a week to lower-income children.

A few days later, my business was open and flourishing. Of

course, that just consisted of me and my Mustang zooming around the hills and pulling up to homes I only dreamed of entering. At the end of the day, reality set back in when I would wind down the hill and return home to the hood.

One day, a neighbor called asking for help in tutoring her son, whom we will call Chucky. He was having difficulty in all subjects. I felt confident I could help and agreed to do so.

The day of our first tutoring session arrived. Chucky knocked on the door with books in hand, and I directed him to the kitchen table. After a brief period of me trying to create a friendly, relaxed environment with a little laughter and a few comforting words, I asked him if he had any homework I could be helpful with. He shook his head, indicating, "No." I then asked him to turn in his math book and show me where they were in class. When he turned to the page, I asked him if he was comfortable with the math problems on the page. He did not respond, so I pointed to the first problem and asked him if he would like to work the problem together. I started with addition. "So here we need to add these two numbers together, so we add twelve plus five and we get…" It was complete silence. After a brief pause, I pretended as though we were both answering and said, "Seventeen, right?" We continued on this path for about an hour until our time was over.

Chucky and I would repeat this rather odd form of exchange. He would come to the session and for one solid hour would say nothing, always with his head down, never looking up from the books. Eventually, I felt maybe it was time to reach out to his mother. So, one day I called and asked his mother if Chucky was quiet at home.

"Yes, he is," she replied.

I told her, "He literally doesn't say a word the whole time he's with me, and I'm not sure I'm really making a difference."

She became rather quiet as she listened to my description of past sessions with Chucky. Her responses were brief and low, as though I was singing a very familiar song that she didn't want to hear. Somewhere during my descriptions I sensed that she ceased listening and was simply waiting for me to finish so she could ask me to keep trying. Sympathizing with her desperation, I told her I would.

Why did I agree to keep trying? What made me think I would be any more successful than I had been in the past few weeks? I did not have any new tricks up my sleeve. I felt as though I had given Chucky's mother a false sense of hope and in the process had overcommitted myself.

What to do? What to do? I never had a child that would not speak. How do you tutor a child that will not talk to you? I just sat for a while and pondered. Maybe my goal was too high and a little off the mark. I was trying to get Chucky to work math problems and read in front of me. Maybe I should focus on creating opportunities for him to view himself in a slightly more positive manner. I thought to myself, *Chucky can always find someone to teach him the information, but how does he find someone to help him enjoy the process of learning so that it continues in my absence?*

I decided that instead of focusing on improving grades directly through the tutoring, I would focus on improving his self-concept and thereby hopefully improve his approach to learning. My hope was that this new strategy would cause him to become more optimistic about the process. Maybe they were baby steps, but it was worth a try. Anything was better than what we were currently doing. Chucky listened, but he still never spoke. Eventually, our tutoring sessions stopped.

Several years later I saw his sister and asked how Chucky was doing. She quickly and enthusiastically replied, "He's doing great! He's a rapper and has a recording contract with a major label."

I looked at her with such surprise on my face as I replied, "Are you talking about *Chucky?*"

She laughed and answered, "Yes, one day he just started

talking and never stopped."

I smiled inside as I realized for the first time that he had something to say all along. It just took a little longer for him to find his voice.

How could I forget my own motto that I spend so much time quoting to everyone else? My motto is, "It's never an issue of whether our thoughts and feelings will be expressed, it is always a matter of how and when." It is an easier journey for some than it is for others, but we all make the trip.

The question that popped into my head regarding Chucky was not whether he would make the trip. Instead, I was curious to know what would be the cost for his journey. I know how hard it was for me to describe my interactions with Chucky as I fought hard not to label him. But I was not sure anyone else would fight quite as hard. I wondered what Chucky's school records said about him. What diagnosis they gave him, what labels they used to describe his behavior or lack thereof as a disorder. Our kids spend a lot of their awake hours in school, which is by its nature an evaluative experience. Those school records tell us and the rest of the world how we perform, what we should and should not be considered capable of doing, how much to trust us with certain tasks, and a litany of other characteristics that significantly define our course in life.

For a kid like Chucky, whose gifts were not obvious and possibly not academic, it is hard to find validation in a system that primarily acknowledges reading, writing, math, and is steeped in verbal skills. Those pesky labels not only come, but they come fast, stay forever, and can define such a big part of who you will become.

I had a situation with my oldest son. I will never forget the first time I heard one of those labels uttered in reference to my child. It came out of the teacher's mouth so fast and smooth I almost missed it. Antonio was in the second grade. Kindergarten was great. First grade was not bad, but he was getting a little bored during class. By the time Antonio was in second grade, he was thoroughly burnt out on the entire educational system and decided he no longer wanted to chase the carrot/grade. You could not scare him with the threat of getting a bad grade, because Antonio did not care. The teachers had to revert to giving him incentives just to get him to finish and turn in his schoolwork. If they bribed Antonio with extra computer time, he would not only finish the work in an instant, he would also usually score an A or A+.

This particular year, Antonio had two teachers that taught his class together. They requested a meeting with me, and at that meeting they proceeded to explain the challenges that were being presented in class by Antonio. I am very much a partner with teachers who are sowing into my children. I arrived for the meeting enthused and looking forward to putting our heads together to come up with remedies for what my son was presenting. I entered the classroom. We said our hellos as they directed me to a table with little chairs, where we sat.

They began by telling me what a wonderful child Antonio was, but that he would not finish his work. Even when they gave him extra time or threatened him with losing part of his recess, he still would not finish his work. One of the teachers began showing obvious signs of compassion for what she thought I might be feeling, which were actually her feelings and not mine at all. As we were all having a great, cordial conversation, one teacher said, "A lot of kids have these kinds of learning dis…"

I was so busy enjoying the interaction we were having during this strategy session that I accidentally interrupted her with a comment about Antonio. However, in the back of my mind a little question mark popped up. I said to myself, *Did I just hear her start to say…? No, she was saying…* I dismissed the moment as simply a mistake in hearing her accurately due to my interruption.

We continued talking, and again, in the most soothing and

understanding voice, she proceeded to comfort me a second time by saying, "A lot of kids have learning disorders like Antonio."

No distractions this time. This was the beginning of a whole new classification for my son. A hard left in his educational trajectory and a new ceiling for what people would believe he is capable of achieving.

I must say, I was proud of myself. I never got upset or raised my voice. I listened to all of their diagnoses regarding Antonio. When they had finished, I replied, "You appear to have diagnosed Antonio so clearly you must have had him formally tested, because from what I can see, I am the only one in the room qualified to give him a diagnosis."

What was previously clear, smooth, comforting language by these two teachers, now incorporated a few stammers and stutters as they began looking back and forth at one another. They replied, "No, we have not had him tested."

I answered, "Oh! I see you have also concluded that Antonio is the problem. I'm wondering if there was ever any consideration for the possibility that you could be the problem? Could it be that your teaching strategies are not able to hold my son's attention, not because he is behind you, but because he is in front of you? Was that ever a consideration?"

After the looks back and forth at one another, they attempted a response that just seemed like it would not put me in a better mood. At the risk of being rude, which I hope you can imagine how much I cared about etiquette in that moment, I interrupted again. "Is it possible to have my son officially tested by the district?"

Their responses came much lower in volume and were much more methodical than when we began. The lead teacher replied, "Umm… Yes, we can arrange for him to be tested."

I loosened my shoulders and relieved some of what I hoped was unrecognizable tension, as choice words were backing up in my throat like a crowded runway at LAX. I replied, "Wonderful! That would be great!"

We finished with friendly, light conversation, and off I went.

That is how subtly these life-changing moments can occur. I honestly do not feel either of Antonio's teachers had any malintent. They were wonderful teachers, and I even enjoyed them personally. Today, my children are a product of wonderfully dedicated teachers who receive too little pay and too little appreciation for the hard work they do. I am a fan, an advocate, and a forever partner of these true heroes.

What makes this story so relevant is the fact that both of Antonio's second grade teachers were dedicated, seasoned, and great with the children. This story shows you that even proficient, astute, and likable teachers can have a misstep that can be life-changing for a child.

The district did test Antonio, and he scored above 99.9 percent. My son was not just gifted—he was highly gifted. The speed and level of a regular class was unable to hold his attention. Los Angeles Unified School District had numerous gifted schools and programs which they call the "GATE" program for the gifted and talented. However, they only had five schools for children who were highly gifted, and Antonio was qualified for all of them. Today, that little, athletic, strong-willed boy enjoys math and science and is studying to make significant technological contributions to the science of sustainable energy. We almost never had the opportunity to benefit from his contributions.

I am talking about the power of categorizing people. Schools are one of the first places where we learn how to categorize and what it feels like to be categorized. It is so ingrained into the system that we oftentimes just line up and simply make the requested and recommended left turns and right turns as we are told.

Much like Chucky and Antonio, we all have many dimensions.

Just because Chucky did not want to speak did not mean he did not have a lot to say. This is one detail of the equation I chose to address in this chapter and did not mention in the beginning of this book. The detail is that our "X" has exponents. It can be "X^2" or "X^6" or "X^{100}." Exponents also are called "powers," because every time the exponent/power is raised, the figure increases exponentially. Exponents represent our dimensions. Our dimensions expand us in ways that are necessary and that are profound.

Humans struggle with this concept. We are always wanting to reduce the amount of information we need to process. That is one reason why, as humans, we spend so much time classifying and categorizing one another. Creating social categories helps us formulate opinions about people when we are too busy and do not have time to meet and get to know them. This is one of the ways we decide who gets to enter our lives, who gets to stay in our lives, who must leave, what role individuals fulfill in our lives, and how far in we will permit access. As you can see, there is some form of a gatekeeper that exists in all of us. However, part of the problem is that when we categorize someone based upon one dimension, we often overlook and/or devalue the other dimensions. Like what we saw with Chucky and Antonio.

These two examples involve children. But this issue is not exclusive to children. In fact, this issue is not exclusive. When someone does a good thing, or a kind thing, or a gracious thing, it does not mean they will not have a moment when they do an irreverent thing. Or if a person is funny and a bit silly, it does not mean they cannot be smart and analytical. There are so many dimensions to who you are. In fact, let me personally own that statement by saying there are so many dimensions that make up the person you see in me, and I am enjoying all of them. What you are experiencing in this book are the ones that I allow to take the lead. I am intricate by design. I am still the girl from the hood and

Dr. Jackson-McCoy all at the same time. The girl from the hood never leaves me, and I never want her to go. She has taught me more than any university ever could. I am unapologetically complex and living in all facets of it—intentionally.

Maybe I had a role in helping Chucky become curious about what life might be like if he dared to speak or took the risk of expressing his thoughts and feelings. Maybe he does not remember me at all. Who knows? More to the point, who cares? What we do know is that somewhere in Chucky's journey he did become curious about the what-ifs. Somewhere in the midst of his curiosity, he began to feel that the risk of remaining silent was greater than the risk of speaking. Or let's flip that. Maybe he felt that the potential rewards of speaking were more compelling and made his commitment to silence the greatest risk of all. Many years later as I was sitting watching a group of inner-city kids playing, I wrote:

> *Some people call me high risk.*
> *Some day you may call me Doctor.*
> *I call myself the hope of the future.*
> *So, don't count me out!*

I think back on my times with Chucky, and my only hope is that he never felt I counted him out.

Imagining, Hoping,
and Speculating

Out Loud

Thirteen:

So, You Want to Have a Conversation?

We live in a technological universe in which
we are always communicating. And yet we
have sacrificed conversation for mere
connection.

—Sherry Turkle

I have watched and, on extremely rare occasions, have participated in conversations in which I and others have broken our golden rule of not discussing controversial topics. You know the ones, topics like politics, religion, race, and the list continues. These rare moments have usually occurred during benign social encounters like at a dinner party, during an office chat, etc. Somehow, in the course of our adamant adherence to the golden rule, a particular moment arrives, and, for whatever reason, we dare to broach a topic universally recognized as a "sensitive" issue.

Our frail confidence in stepping into those treacherous waters is usually emboldened by our momentary compulsion to expand someone's perspective on the topic. Fueled by optimism, we brave those waters believing we could succeed in our ambitious endeavor. Our courage in taking the leap is propelled by our belief that good intentions and a commitment to civility will be enough for us to survive the anticipated minefield we are preparing to enter. We charge forward believing we will conclude with our reputations and relationships intact.

So many of these conversations seem to begin the same way. There is that cautiously optimistic initial phase when one person makes a statement and the other person eagerly chimes in to concur. The fleeting enjoyment that comes from their agreement is often premature, but eagerly welcomed none the less. Typically, at this point, you are simply validating each other's vague language that espouses some universally accepted truth that no one on the planet would disagree with on face value. Statements like, "There's just too much going on in the world today," or the famous, "We need to come together" or the even more famous, "It is important to be able to have a conversation."

At this point, the conversation is still at an altitude of 30,000 feet so everyone is continuing to use the same word choices in their statements. This phase feels good. However, at this point, we are only exchanging words. No one has ascribed any conclusive or dissenting meaning to those words. As a result, that good feeling begins to breed a sense of hope or maybe just a greater level of comfort in moving further down the road on this issue. Suddenly, one of you is compelled to take a deeper dive and drop the altitude to enter the second phase of this discourse. We are still agreeing and exchanging innocuous language except now the other person has taken the bold step of offering a small addition to your statement. There is no getting around it. This addition we are waiting to hear is the first step in unveiling their theory of either which road they believe will get us where we want to go or reveal who gets left behind on the journey. At 30,000 feet everything in eyes view is simply revealing a sea of shapes and colors. As you lower the altitude suddenly you begin to distinguish the details of the land. The vast chasm that exists between what you meant by those words and what I meant by those words is beginning to reveal itself even if not in its entirety. I can see enough to realize that we are not even on the same planet not to mention being on the same page. This realization becomes the impetus for the next phase.

In the next phase we are still cordial and appropriately turn-taking in our dialogue as we strive to hear and to be heard. However, the language is stronger although delivered in the same calm respectful voice. You know the voice. That relaxed voice intended to communicate that we are still listening and respecting one another despite the differences in our opinions. The real function of that voice is to mask how hard we are working to contain any semblance of the negative emotions that are bubbling to the surface in what is becoming a slowly incinerating discussion.

At this point we are still clinging (if only by a fingernail) to our commitment of respecting one another's differences of opinion. You are still listening, however, every reply begins with a standard affirming sentence prior to decimating the person's argument. Something like, "That's a good point, however…" or "I see what you're saying but what comes to my mind is…" or the all-powerful ultimate affirming preface, "That's a good point, I agree with you on that point, but the bigger issue is…" and the list goes on. If we were to take a moment to look beyond the surface of our assertions and assumptions, you will quickly discover that we are disagreeing about more than "where we want to go." We are disagreeing about who gets to go, and what road should be taken to get there. It makes perfect sense that you would choose a snow-laden road as the perfect path if you are sitting in a brand-new high-powered snowmobile. But, if I am standing with just my tennis shoes looking at that snow-laden road, it makes sense that I would disagree regarding that being the perfect path for all of us. Unfortunately, equality is still a goal and thus far equity is still an experiment that apparently not everyone believes is a good idea. Welcome to the conversation!

One of the main topics we disagree on is the extent to which we believe we could agree given that many of us are not listening anymore. It is oftentimes hard to hear when you are fighting so hard for the right to be heard. Who wants the burdensome task of listening? At this point, the real privileges being vied for are interjections and interruptions. If you happen to be in one of those benign social encounters I was mentioning, then the real goal is to interject using polite interruptions. You want to preface your next assertion with a statement that acknowledges the interruption without owning the rudeness associated with it. "…I didn't mean to interrupt, I just wanted to mention that…" The communicative creativity displayed in the exchange is on steroids.

One day I was listening to an announcer referee a boxing match and I thought there was an uncanny similarity between the conversations I had witnessed and participated in and what was happening in that boxing ring. Each person enters the conversation knowing their advantages and disadvantages. "In the blue corner weighing in at 180 pounds… and in the red corner, weighing in at 185…" The statement, "I understand what you're saying. The only point I want to make is…" Interpreted in boxing language they are in essence saying, "We want a good clean fight." The match begins, "Cynthia really came out fighting and dominated the first round. However, towards the end of the round Susan delivered a solid one-two punch that took the wind out of Cynthia for a moment. In round 2 Cynthia is making a comeback and is on the attack, but Susan lands a strong right hook by surprise and follows with the knockout punch. Cynthia struggles but manages to get to her feet…"

There is a bit of comedy in it. What is less comical is the fact that these thoughts and opinions inform our actions. On the other side of our actions ("X") we will always find our impact on the lives of others ("Y").

The most intense moments of the encounter arise in our push to define and/or strongly influence the narrative. This is the part of the process that people seldom want to acknowledge because the goal has shifted. The goal is no longer to listen, consider, or explore. Now, the goal is to win. My concern regarding this shift is that if I feel justified in not listening, I no longer need to consider the fact that you might have something of value to offer. If I am no longer listening to anything except all the ways in which we differ, I have eliminated all the possible categories I could place you in with the exception of one – my opposition, or more plainly stated – a problem. Now, my stance is fully justified. My actions represent my effort to protect myself and others from all the ways I conceive of you being a threat either in thought or in deed. I "need" to stop listening. I "need" to cease giving value to what you have to say. I "need" to protect myself from all the ways that you are a danger to what I believe. Suddenly, my fright and flight responses are not only justified, they are also deemed necessary. The inability to consider that there is any part of the issue that the two sides agree upon and the unwillingness to use their agreement as a starting point is Kryptonite to the conversation.

Too often, those focused on identifying and classifying their adversaries are the ones that play a significant role in defining the narratives we wake up and experience as today's reality. In life, there does come that moment when it is time to fight. There are moments when it is time to stand up for what you believe in. My concern arises when we become so distracted by swinging and throwing theoretic rhetorical punches at one another that we fail to realize the point in which the injuries are so great on both sides that no one wins.

What I have been saying is that having a conversation is easy. The hard part is getting to the place where we can. We don't live in the courts, so it is hard to strike it from the record. Actually, it is impossible to strike something from the record in or out of court. You can only remove it from paper. The real record is being kept in our hearts and minds. That is where seeds germinate, and where roots grow. Sometimes the roots are of things like bitterness, and other times they serve as the foundation for how we will strengthen ourselves and others towards positive change. It all depends on what we allow to be planted and what we choose to water.

Another reality about the things we are fighting for is that even when you fight alone you want to feel that you have people on your side. People who believe that you are justified in what you are fighting for. So now, the fighter has another goal to achieve. They must make sure people understand why the fight matters. If you are fighting for one of those "universal truths" that's easy. You pretty much have everyone on your side. If the rationale for your fight is a harder sell, now you need "tactics." After all, you are still trying to win. Here we go down the next very classic road to winning a fight: intimidate your opponent and create fear in the onlookers. At this stage you want to communicate to onlookers that the prize you are fighting for is so important for everyone that their greatest fear would be that you would lose.

I try to never live in fear. Instead, I strive to live in awareness, conviction, and moving in the direction of what I believe to be positive change. I champion the commitment and engagement of others who are doing the same. Agreeing with me is not a prerequisite for me to appreciate you. What I appreciate most is the passion and engagement someone has the courage to demonstrate when fighting for their truths regardless of whether they neatly align with mine. However, just because I do not require agreement does not mean I am without prerequisites. My appreciation is reserved for those that maintain respect and empathy for others as fundamental principles in achieving their goals and fighting for what they believe.

Fear, when used as a tool to enlist others, can be so divisive. It dichotomizes the world into groups of friends and foe, who gets to stay, and who must go. Sometimes we allow a few people to change ranks. Those that seem to defy many of the traits we have ascribed to their category. Interestingly, these individuals are often viewed as "different" rather than providing a moment when we question the validity of our assumptions regarding the group.

When I think of what ignites fear in me, it is that we would lose interest in continuing our struggle to achieve that conversation. All the awkward and difficult moments that one experiences in arriving at a place of having genuine dialogue that is purposeful and bigger than the individuals that are speaking. Even more frightening than our own apathy is the thought that our lack of engagement would become the legacy we leave to our children. If, based upon our own disengagement and polarization for those with whom we disagree, we send the message to our children that the discourse no longer matters, we will have committed the greatest disservice of all.

The thought that the challenges of exploring the vast chasms that often exist between us would end our exchange at the initial cautiously optimistic phase would be unfortunate. We only experience these challenges when people still care enough to endure the discomforts of the process. My concern is that we would no longer feel the conversation matters or is possible. Deafening silence is my greatest fear.

I must admit that I am speaking to everyone except those whom we refer to as Generation Z (aka Gen Z). These are individuals between 8 and 23 years of age.

We understand those referred to as "Gen Z" do not represent a monolith. They vary in many ways. However, we also recognize some characteristics in this population that are uniquely prevalent enough to, at a minimum, suggest tendencies. Generally speaking, Gen Z is highly informed and unafraid of being vocal regarding "sensitive" issues. They have information at their fingertips and are not afraid to use it or to change it. They have managed to move past the filters that define traditional narratives in order to create their own. Not only are they accessing astonishing amounts of information, they are bolstering their knowledge by exposing themselves to experiences. While everyone else is following news, Gen Z is following culture, engaged in dialogue, and defining their own narratives that often occur so quickly that it is over and done before everyone else gets their daily news. Gen Z is in no way waiting for the perfect opportunity or reason to initiate a conversation. They are having bold and vibrant conversations about any and every topic others question whether to discuss. They are proof that the conversation is possible and is happen with or without the rest of us.

Fourteen:

What If Hypotheticals Came True?

Never doubt that a small group of
thoughtful, committed citizens can
change the world; indeed, it is the only
thing that ever has.

—Margaret Mead

My youngest child was diagnosed with autism. I remember the
state of the world when he was first diagnosed. At least, the state
of the world as it appeared from my point of view. All the stares
and dirty looks that Jackson and I received. Wherever we went,
Jackson was either too loud, too emotional, too active, on the floor
having a full-blown tantrum, or a combination of all four. I wanted
so much for people to understand what we were going through
and to have compassion on Jackson. Actually, I was hoping they
would have compassion for both of us. I needed it as much as
Jackson, since I was often on the floor as much as he was, trying
to move him past the tantrum. When I think back to those days,
there was one incident that is most memorable.

We were driving down the 405 freeway during Los Angeles
rush hour traffic. It was pure gridlock, with speeds up to no more
than five miles per hour. Worst of all, we were between exits, and
Jackson, who was 6 years old at the time, informed me that he had
to use the restroom—bad! Unable to exit the freeway, I pulled to

the shoulder of the road and allowed him to urinate on the passenger side of the car away from the view of motorists.

A few weeks later we were in the grocery store parking lot, loading groceries into the car. Suddenly, Jackson informed me that he had to use the restroom. I placed the last grocery bag in the back of the car, took Jackson's hand and proceeded toward the store. Jackson immediately pulled back on my arm while frantically repeating, "I have to go! I have to go!" He was pulling me back toward the car. Finally, he broke away from my hand, ran beside the car, pulled his pants down, and began to urinate as though we were back on the 405 freeway. This is one of those mama moments when you realize that you taught your child something you did not want them to learn, then forgot to correct the error by unteaching.

Well, all that hindsight was of little effect as I tried desperately to stop Jackson. But it was too late. Jackson had achieved a full stream. I then did the only thing left to do which was to cover him while he finished. As we were standing there waiting for this to be over, two matured ladies returned to their car, which was parked next to us. They looked at us with sheer disgust and did not fail to throw in a few verbal statements to support their dirty looks. I understood how we must have looked and simply held my silence as they told us how we were repulsive. After a few of their comments, I took advantage of their pause and said, "I'm so sorry, he doesn't mean any harm. He's autistic."

They couldn't care less. All they knew was that they were disgusted by the sight, and they continued to tell me so in no uncertain terms. Somewhere in the midst of their continued looks and comments, they had arrived at that place my mom would always mention as being her "last nerve." I never knew where it was, or whether she knew the exact location, but everybody knew when they had landed on her "last nerve." Well, these two unfortunate women had landed on mine! I am sure you could finish the story from here. Like lightning, I transitioned out of the role of the understanding citizen and transformed into that other personality that every mother carries, ready to whip out like a cowboy draws his gun for a gun fight. Mama Grizzly had arrived with a fierce growl.

The tables had definitely turned as I inquired regarding how long they intended to stand there looking and pointing at my son's private parts; I accused them of being sick, old perverts looking for an excuse to stare; and then I began walking toward them as I accused them of being the ones with the problem and offered to help them work it out. The two ladies quickly entered their car, locked their doors, and took off. But the nagging feelings they left me to ponder and rehearse continued to replay in my heart and mind for years to come. Every time I relived the incident in my head it made me feel so bad, so misrepresented, and so powerless. I felt powerless, because in that moment there was nothing I could do to evoke or redirect compassion or understanding toward my little boy. A little boy that was using all the energy he had just to make it through the next five minutes without an incident he would regret. And, although he oftentimes could not stop himself from creating embarrassing moments, he was aware enough to feel every consequence of being humiliated. What a life!

As I reminisce on days gone by, my thoughts also take me to the day in 2005 when I was watching the *Today Show* and heard the announcement that Suzanne and Bob Wright had started an organization for children diagnosed with autism. This organization was designed to fund global biomedical research focused on the causes, prevention, treatments, and cure for autism; to raise public awareness about autism and its effects on individuals, families, and society; and to bring hope to all who deal with the hardships of this disorder. To moms like myself, this was amazing news! Somebody out there powerful enough to have a voice you could hear across the country was coming to help us. I must be honest.

I do not know much about the organization. My focus was in no way directed toward the organization. My attention was laser-focused on Suzanne and Bob Wright. My question was, "How are they going to pull this off?" My hope was that they would succeed.

I would peek in on their progress as the months went by. It did not appear that they were finding a cure. I did not hear of any breakthroughs on understanding the cause of autism. But while I was focused on cures and causes, I failed to notice how subtly things were changing around us. The world actually began to feel like a different place for Jackson and me. We did not receive the same curious looks. They had been replaced with smiles and "how-do-you-do's" from passersby, and it felt wonderful!

I do not think Suzanne and Bob ever found the cause or a cure for autism. I am sure someone would have mentioned that groundbreaking news had it occurred. But what they did achieve was one of the most powerful accomplishments of all. From me and Jackson's perspective, it was the second best achievement to having a cure. Suzanne and Bob managed to plant a seed and enlist an army that was strong enough and loud enough to galvanize a country. With the help of that growing army, they managed to take what was nothing more than a hypothetical notion of creating an atmosphere of tolerance and compassion and made it our reality.

A few years later, Jackson and I went to a restaurant with some friends. I picked up Jackson after he finished a fun-filled day with Grandma. Little did I know that one of the highlights of his time with Grandma involved a big bowl of sugar-filled chocolate ice cream. For someone like Jackson, that bowl of delicious sugary dessert was lethal.

The restaurant was crowded, and the wait was long. In the waiting area, all the seats were filled, so we stood along the wall. Finally, a few spaces became available on a nearby bench. I noticed Jackson getting a little fidgety. Grandma's ice cream/sugar factory was kicking in. Since Jackson had started dancing, I thought it might help him relax if we sit. So, we decided to claim those available seats.

While I was tending to Jackson, I could not help but notice the demeanor of the woman sitting next to me. It is a little odd to describe, but she was clearly annoyed by the fact that we were even in the building. That is not what was odd to me. What was odd was the fact that although she didn't like Jackson's fidgeting, most of her focus was on communicating that she was holding on to her section of the bench and would not move one inch to accommodate anyone sitting next to her, least of all Jackson and me. Of course, given that no one was asking her to relinquish any of her prime real estate on the bench, the whole interaction was strange and a bit silly to say the least. I turned to her, hoping to bring a little sensibility to the moment, and said, "My apologies, Jackson is autistic."

The woman was so entrenched in the warfare she had going that not only did she not care about what I was saying, she refused to even acknowledge that I was talking to her. She just continued looking straight ahead with a stiff neck like an Army recruit trying to pass inspection. Although Jackson was working hard to fight the sugar rush and was doing a great job maintaining himself, it was clear to me that neither Jackson nor I could be nice enough to change her thinking or her prayer that we would just go away.

That is what made the moment so wonderful for me. Suddenly, I realized that it was okay, because today she was the exception, when a few years ago her behavior would have been the rule. This woman caught me off-guard because it had been a few years since I had experienced that level of intolerance toward Jackson. WOW! What a difference a few years can make! I immediately pictured Suzanne and Bob Wright when they first announced the organization with all their grand ideas about changing the world. It was clear that Suzanne and Bob made a tangible change in the world, although not without the help of millions of others. What started as a seed, planted by two people we had never met, resulted in sweeping changes across the country that Jackson and I were benefiting from and feeling every day.

Time had passed. Jackson and I were basking in the support and acceptance we were experiencing from what seemed to be coming from everywhere. However, I was totally unprepared to discover that systems did not necessarily follow the trends and tendencies of people. School systems, to be exact, still just saw my child as an extra burden, with no time or interest in helping him learn. One school sat Jackson next to a child and gave Jackson permission to copy him. In another school, I kept wondering why there was no homework. The teacher, who continually lamented about this being her last year teaching, said she would be retiring, told me she wanted families to be able to enjoy time together and not have to worry about homework. All the work was done in class. When I requested copies of Jackson's classwork near the end of the year, there were a total of three sheets of paper.

I knew it was time for a different plan, but what do you do, and where do you go? I looked at Jackson and said, "There are a lot of kids just like you that cannot speak for themselves. You and I will fight to make a difference for you and all the other kids that need someone to speak up for them too."

Jackson said, "Okay."

In case you have not tried it, fighting systems is hard, painful, and not for the faint of heart. They fight back with teeth! It definitely felt like David versus Goliath. But, if I recall the story correctly, David won!

Long story short, we won the bigger battle on behalf of other kids. We managed to bring scrutiny and greater accountability to the schools in question. But what about Jackson and me? We still had no answer for ourselves. There I was, sitting at home in what began to feel like sheer hopelessness. Jackson and I had been strong warriors for so long. Yet here we were struggling to find, feel, or tap into our own superpowers. I could not find help for my son. All I could find were beautiful brochures of services and places that turned out to be highly overrated and self-aggrandized. I also found more than my share of well-dressed administrators who had the most eloquent and creative ways of telling us that Jackson did not qualify for their services.

One autism school we applied for had the usual bot with the nice voice who had us jump through tons of hoops just so she could check off the boxes on her fiduciary list before telling us what she knew the moment we first walked in the door—"He doesn't fit the type of students we accept." Unable to remove the perplexed look from my face, the woman said, "There is a program that your son qualifies to attend. We can walk over, and you can take a look." Jackson and I were so happy. We took off, following her as she walked us over to another section of the campus. We arrived, and she informed us that this was the school.

Jackson and I just stood there speechless, as his smile disappeared. and so did mine. Jackson looked up at me as if to say, "Mama, you're not leaving me here, are you?"

Tears began to stream down my face. The tears fell not because the kids were so low-functioning. The tears fell because it was clear to me that these were the kids no one believed would ever have a real contribution or become more advanced than they were in that moment. They were being managed and entertained but not sown into. The main thing I was looking for was someone who would believe in my son. Someone who would look at him and see all the possibilities I saw. And, yes, I saw them clearly. This place was the absolute antithesis of what I was hoping for. I thanked her for her time and left.

It felt like life had backed Jackson and me into a corner. In fact, we could no longer see our path or a way out. Until one day when I became sick and tired of being sick and tired. Mama Grizzly began to rise again. With a perilous growl, I determined that it would be a rough day for somebody, but a good day for us. This was my Shawanda moment all over again. The woman pressed against the wall in despair rose with a world of possibilities and hope again. As I thought back to the story of David and Goliath, I said to myself, *Goliath may have been big and intimidating, but David won by being precise and strategic.* I realized in that moment that although I may have been limited in my own personal skill set, I was not limited in my reach. Yes, I definitely felt life's thumb pushing on my chest—hard. For a moment I had forgotten that I have the ability to push back—hard. I remember telling a friend that I did not want to wait until the thumb was lifted. I wanted to show my children that you rise despite the thumb in your chest.

The second thing I understood in that moment was that sometimes pushing back and leaning in means going outside of yourself and getting to just the right stranger. Someone who sees the land that is so intimidating to you, and, from their vantage point, views that same land as nothing more than their familiar battlefield. I wanted to reach out and get a warrior that had been trained with surgical precision in using thoughts, strategies, and abilities I did not even know existed. Someone who would be able to stay ten steps ahead of where I was thinking, simply because they knew the backroads to places where I cannot even find the turnoffs.

When I rose, my growl came in the form of Google. The way I saw it, if I could type in a search bar, nothing and no one was out of my reach. You may ask, "What did you type in the search bar?" I typed, "Most powerful attorney in the world." I was not looking for the most powerful in the city, or the county, or the state, or even the country. I was settling for nothing less than the most powerful attorney in the world! I was looking for David packaged in the form of Goliath! And, yes, I found her!

Her name was Diane Cafferata. Barely five feet tall, gentle on the eye, brilliant, with a slightly exposed heart. So, who was this newfound stranger? Well, when you are sitting at home watching TV or checking your news app for the day's latest and greatest and you hear about cases being fought for and against some of the largest companies in the world, that's Diane. But apparently there was more to this esteemed stranger than I realized, because when I called, she picked up the phone and answered. I was calling her, yet totally unprepared to speak to her. I was braced for battling my way through a long line of receptionists, assistants, paralegals, and wonderfully engaging voicemails telling me to leave my number and someone will get back with me as soon as possible. I was prepared, geared up, and girded for everything except for Diane Cafferata to answer her phone. What powerful attorney answers their phone?

These are the moments in life that confuse me. I was always taught that you work hard so you can afford to layer people in front of you so you become harder and harder to access. The more money you make, the harder you are to reach, until you get to the place where only "important" people with as much money as you can successfully break through the barriers. No one told me anything about answering your own phone. It kind of messes up the model in an amazingly wonderful and refreshing way.

What you may not realize in this story is how much time had passed between me receiving three sheets of paper representing Jackson's year of work, and the moment when I called Diane. The reason Jackson and I were so worn down was because years had passed, and we had become weary. Through these years, as we homeschooled, Jackson's language began to manifest. Such a trooper! Jackson never gave up, and he insisted that I not give up either, no matter how hard it was or what the day would throw at him. He kept wanting to learn, wanting to grow, wanting to be, as he called it, "regular." The tantrums stopped, and his thoughts began to find their way out just enough where I could see glimpses of what was inside this young man. All those years I kept telling professionals that my son was smart and was having great thoughts. He just did not know how to let them out. It became increasingly clear to me over the years that helping that process happen was my job!

Although "attorney" was one of the words in my Google search, I was not just looking for an attorney. I could find one of those anywhere. I was surrounded by good attorneys. What I was looking for and was determined to find was someone who was proficient and surgical with their voice and their choice. Someone that aligned with what Jackson and I believed were possibilities for his life.

Diane is not only an attorney at one of the most powerful law firms in the world; she is also a partner. She got busy working and wielding her brilliance as though Jackson was her own. Every weapon in her arsenal that allowed her to change the world for this little boy, she put into effect.

Today, Diane and I are best friends, enjoying restaurants, and shopping for wonderful pastas and pesto. My forever friend, we are two souls who were destined to collide. What we share is so genuine, so heartfelt. I guess I have a small glimpse of the comradery soldiers feel when they return home. You never forget the person that was willing to walk on the battlefield with you. Today our friendship is about more than Jackson. I am no longer the mom of the boy who has tantrums and cannot speak. I am the mom of a teenager that is going to dances, laughing with friends, and asking for a car. He labels his unique manner, "My personality."

It is funny, because at the time I was just a mom who had run out of answers for my son, and Diane was my pit bull. She did not know I was Dr. Jackson-McCoy, and I did not know she could make a killer marinara sauce. All I knew was that she was the perfect person to change the world. From the moment she walked into our lives, my son's life and mine were never the same again.

I began to think, if Suzanne and Bob could change the world once, and Diane could change the world the second time, could we possibly change it again? What if someone else, other than Suzanne, Bob, or Diane, woke up one day and believed the world could be different, hypothetically speaking, of course.

And what if that someone happened to be you? Be clear, I am not talking about you sponsoring or heading a big organization. Organizations are nice, but there is nothing more powerful than a "movement," because a movement happens one person at a time. It was not the organization that made the difference for Suzanne and Bob in the early days. It was their ability to create a movement that swept across the country and enlisted the hearts of individuals, one human being at a time. Unfortunately, the major barrier we face with movements is that most of us are trained to associate movements with specific causes. Something encapsulated enough to wrap our minds around like feeding hungry children, educating the disenfranchised, providing shelter for the homeless, etc.

But what if the cause was just "us"? Hypothetically speaking, of course. It just feels too big, too nebulous, too ill-defined. But think about it. Compared to so many other causes, having a broader topic to embrace, like "us," should come much more naturally and provide greater opportunities for involvement. After all, we've all been one, known one, and have been touched by one. Maybe that is the problem. Maybe this cause is so vast and so close to all of us that it is just too difficult to see clearly and feel empowered enough to make a difference.

I told one story that was about two people (Suzanne and Bob) who made a difference for a nation. The second story was about a woman who made a difference for a boy and his mother. Drastically different, yet equally as powerful. This is what I was telling you in chapter one regarding the equation "If X were true, what would it mean for Y?" We see here that "X" and "Y" are interchangeable; as I was "X" for Jackson, I was "Y" for Diane. If you recall, the other point I made in chapter one was about outside influences and how they all have different magnitudes but equal significance in the equation. You may want to check back to chapter one for a refresher, but I talked about how "X" and "Y" can be influenced by "W" or "Z." You can see these principles manifesting in these stories. Suzanne and Bob started something. But it was outside influences that carried the heart of the message across the country so profoundly that one day Jackson and I looked up and the world had changed. This was nothing different from what Diane was able to do as she used her power and weight to move heaven and earth for her youngest client. Ultimately, they both changed the world by mobilizing and working in unison with the forces and influences of "W" and "Z."

Although Diane and I are good friends, she only recently found out that I was writing a book, and she was surprised to find out that she is in it. She called the other day for our scheduled Zoom tea together. As we were celebrating her amazing new book for corporate executives, I dropped this bomb on her. Not knowing what her reaction would be, I was so happy and relieved to find that all she could say is, "I never knew what it meant to you until now." Sometimes we understand that our "X" is a good thing, and we may have some level of insight into the fact that it is a powerful thing. But we may not understand all the ways in which it is a life-changing thing in the lives of others.

No one has ever heard this story until now. It feels so good to finally speak about the details out loud and to tell the story about this amazing woman who came into my life at the most opportune moment and gave both Jackson and me something to believe in again.

Sometimes our role is nothing more than to help someone else believe again. Not just believe, but believe enough to personally send a message that is strong enough and loud enough for your son, daughter, neighbor, husband, wife, or friend, or more simply stated, for "us" to actually wake up one day and feel that change has come.

Once we silence our inner critic, the part that constantly reminds us of what we cannot do, what is too hard, and what will take too long, then and only then will we discover, and in some instances rediscover, our own ability to make hypotheticals come true.

Fifteen

The Great Awakening

Why have I written a chapter about awakenings? I wrote this chapter because on the other side of awakenings we often find our voice which is the heart of what this book is about. It is our voice and our choice that we have been talking about. So much of this book is about what matters to me. It is your voice and your choices that announce to the world what matters to you. Oftentimes, you hear people talk about wanting to *find their voice*. Beware! Feeling that you have not found your voice does not mean you are not making statements every day, even if they are revealed through your silence.

As I write those words and say them aloud to myself my thoughts take me back to one of my high school teachers. She was a young, beautiful, powerhouse that led with compassion, and had a way of making everyone she met feel as powerful as she saw herself. At barely five feet tall and not quite 100 pounds she entered our lives, and the rest is history.

I remember her teaching a group of us a song that we performed for the entire school with funky choreography. The lyrics of the song were the words to the preamble of the Constitution. In all my years of schooling and history classes requiring us to study aspects of the Constitution, and scoring high marks on history tests, this was the first time I was listening to the preamble and paying attention. By the way, she did not teach history. She was an English and drama teacher. But more than an English and drama teacher, she was a person that was very aware of her "X" and the ways in which she could and wanted to impact "Y."

Of all the things I remember about her, what I remember most was how she spoke about great inventors from the past with such excitement and intrigue that it was almost as though they still walked among us. When she spoke of them, her focus was not on their inventions, it was on their life, their journey, who they were as individuals, how their choices contributed to all the ways they were able to make a positive difference, and the personal sacrifice they often had to endure for doing so. The person she was most enthralled with was Isaac Newton. Her excitement about him was infectious. After only a few of her anecdotes about him, I found myself at the bookstore purchasing a book about the life of Isaac Newton. I was captivated by his story, his brilliance, his mistakes, his perspective on life, and his sacrifice. I anticipated every next page to learn more. This was my first time hearing his quotes. Some of them reverberate with me until this day. My favorite quote from Isaac Newton is: "If I have seen further, it is by standing on the shoulders of giants."

Yes, she was an English and drama teacher. But if that is the main image you have of her from my story, you missed the heart of what kept her alive in my memory and why I am still talking about her decades later. She was a woman that searched for, had experienced, and was constantly in pursuit of awakenings for herself and for every person within her reach. This was a woman committed to positively impacting the lives of others even if only by her own definition.

Her tenure at the school was relatively short. But it was just long enough to change my life. Before she left, she wrote me a note. She ended the note by saying, "…there is so much more I wanted to share with you. But I know you are curious, and you will find it on your own."

Why did I find so much enjoyment in reading about the life of Isaac Newton? What I was enjoying most had less to do with Isaac Newton and more to do with this being my first time feeling so much curiosity. My teacher was right. I had become curious and that curiosity was being unleashed full throttle. It felt amazing!

As awakenings go, not only was my teacher a person that was not afraid to look, she was determined to keep looking. She desired to be awake and stay awake.

Through my own journey I have learned, the two most powerful forces that guide us to our awakenings are curiosity and discomfort. It is curiosity that moves us into engagement and discomfort that keeps us pursuing better days.

I appreciate that my teacher did not spend all of her time thinking and rethinking her thoughts about herself. Although I recognize those introspective reflections have a place and purpose in all our lives. Instead, she balanced the time she spent discovering and clarifying her truths with the time she spent sharing with those willing to receive what she was willing to offer. Out of all that she offered, maybe what I appreciate most is what she never offered. My teacher never offered answers.

There are so many answers I do not have and that we do not have. So much of what we purport is based on the subjective landscape of our perspective. That perspective only serves as an answer for those who find alignment or an attraction to what is being purported. In time, what I have come to value most is not the person that seems to have the answers. Instead, my greatest admiration goes to the person that generates the greatest questions, is curious enough to pursue them, and cultivates an atmosphere that breeds new knowledge by provoking curiosity in others.

That is what my teacher did so consistently and effortlessly. She provoked curiosity which is what ignites the brilliance that is in all of us. It is that brilliance that helps navigate us to our own version of answers.

Society tends to rank order topics. That means some of us will feel our brilliance more or less than others depending on in which topic we excel. Sadly, so many of us sit with our brilliance waiting for someone to come by and believe in us enough that we would be convinced to believe in ourselves. Why wait for someone to believe in you. You be the first believer and believe in yourself.

Since we are on the subject, there is something else I want to mention. I notice how we talk about awakenings as if we know what they are. I am guilty of doing the same. When I say the word "awakening" I know the essence of what I mean. Others have a sense for the general meaning of what I am attempting to imply. It is confusing.

I think to some degree, on this topic, we all just assume we know what each other is implying. However, the question is still sitting in the middle of the room like a big green elephant. What qualifies as an awakening? Is it when some issue that has felt so distant from you suddenly arrives at your doorstep and compels you to, at a minimum, acknowledge its existence if not its relevance? Maybe awakenings have levels. Maybe the most authentic or impactful awakenings are the ones that arrive due to a long emotional or intellectual journey. Maybe authenticity and impact are less important than whether the awakening is sustainable. Or maybe one cannot happen without the other.

Also, I wonder about time. In some ways, I think all awakenings take time. Maybe there are instances when we believe our awakening happened in a quick meaningful moment because we only recognized the moment we awakened and did not give credit to all the people and moments whose contribution helped get us there.

As I continue this litany of thoughts and observations, let me also mention that I have noticed some people report being awakened and still feel no call to action. Can you be awakened and just observe or if you only observe are you not fully awake? I do not know the answers to these questions. Neither have I spent an extensive amount of time trying to find the answers or struggling with the true meaning of an awakening. Some are still debating the definition. Others are skipping the debate and offering their version of a definition. Yet, despite the apparent lack of clarity regarding what is an awakening, I believe in them. I always recognize the moment they arrive, and I believe they have value for all of us.

As I jump into this arena and offer a definition of my own, please know that what I am offering are insights into my own views. My statements are not intended to serve as definitive answers for everyone or anyone other than me. As I continue to evolve, so might my definitions. I remain open to that wonderful fact and welcome it.

For me, an awakening happens when I become aware at a level that is deeper than where my mind alone can take me. My yearning for these defining encounters is compelled by my effort to find greater alignment between what is in my head, what is in my heart, and what is in my soul. For me, that alignment is like air. I need it to breathe. That alignment is where I find my balance and stability. My quest for awakenings is further fueled by my quest for authenticity in the areas where I have difficulty convincing myself of what does not feel like my truth.

For all the reasons I mentioned above, the question I constantly pose to myself is not "What is an awakening?" My question is "How do I position myself to ensure that I am experiencing what I believe them to be." My goal in writing this chapter is to share a few of my thoughts regarding the context in which I believe these amazing phenomena occur.

I see life as presenting the opportunity for us to experience three types of awakenings: Intrapersonal, interpersonal, and systemic. Intrapersonal awakenings create a greater self-awareness. Interpersonal awakenings reveal greater insights regarding the relationships we form with others. The third type is what I call systemic. These awakenings reveal insights regarding policies, procedures, and practices that impact our lives and the lives of others.

As I continue to journey across and within all three types of awakenings, I have amassed lessons learned. One of the lessons I learned is that some of the most painful stories that result from our failure to wake up will not be told by us. They will be told by those whose lives and livelihoods are dependent on whether we wake up and decide to look beyond our own comfort zone.

Many years ago, I conducted a study and found that when individuals are told about someone in distress, even if the cause of the distress is due to something they define as a taboo, their response was to express compassion and concern. Ultimately, what the study revealed was that when people differed in their beliefs, the challenge was not getting them to care about one another's distress. The challenge was getting them to care long enough to make a difference. Sustained caring was our obstacle to overcome. Their caring and sense of engagement did not continue beyond our conversation on the topic. It is true, most people need a reason to care. It can come from having a similar experience, like having a loved one affected by the same situation. Maybe they saw something in the news and could not get it out of their head. Whatever the impetuses may be for choosing to care, I celebrate the choice.

I mention this study because as I look back, I realize that through this study which addressed *engagement* and *caring*, I was actually asking the world, "What will it take for you to wake up and get involved in the issues that matter to me?" Although I was disappointed by some of their answers, I understood their response. These were not people who did not care. These were people who did not care as deeply about the things that mattered to me. They gave me the same response I probably would have given them if the topic were distant from what I have chosen to be passionate about.

Sometimes things occur that are in such opposition to our principles, values, and beliefs that it not only gets our attention, but it also creates just enough discomfort to keep us from settling back into our familiar settings, patterns and mindsets. In some ways it was a bit unrealistic of me to expect more from the study than what it delivered. Awakenings are not always moments when we suddenly see the picture. They are often moments when we realize there is a picture that needs to be seen. My study did not measure or account for that outcome.

In taking a lesson from my high school teacher, maybe the best we can do is continue choosing to "look" and "listen," whether it is for ourselves, our loved ones, or those people and issues that exist outside our current topic of interest. And let me not overlook the most common factor we have yet to discuss.

As is often the case with humans, our struggle to see and hear is frequently impeded by our battle to see past our own defenses that are blocking our view. No need to point fingers. We all are guilty of participating at one point or another. The question is not whether you participate in the behavior. The question is, "Which one is your 'go to' move?" Maybe you use denial to pretend it is not there. If we can just deny the existence of the problem, we can avoid unpleasant realities by staying in what we believe to be our comfort zone. Maybe your "go to" move is acceptance. You see the situation without attempting to change it. Or maybe avoidance is your preferred strategy. You do not want to upset the apple cart so you avoid any action that would trigger painful or stressful thoughts or feelings. There are others we could mention. The point is that sometimes we are choosing to do everything except the one thing that will yield greater awareness, which is to look and acknowledge the need for change.

In those moments we are looking but we are still unable to see. We do not always know what we have been missing, but half of the battle is won if we can become curious enough to decide we need to find out.

I believe, in many instances, we are incorrect in our frequent assumption that many people do not see the issues. Oftentimes, it is not that people do not see, it is that when they look, they do not see what you see. There's that pesky issue of perspective again! A frustrating fact of life.

As I mentioned, perspective is powerful. It is the lens through which we view and define reality. The images we attempt to see are colored by what we allow to feed our perspective. A note of caution: the well you drink from matters.

In moments when I fail to see clearly or have chosen to see differently, I am always grateful for those who take what they may view as a *misstep* on my part and count it to my head and not to my heart. I am even more grateful for those who just don't count it. Instead of spending time focused on judging intent and creating attributions, they focus on educating and fostering greater awareness in others.

Today I am a product of time and seasoning. I have learned that, simply by their nature, awakenings espouse discomfort because they require our fantasies to be broken. Humans are highly creative so we often will build another fantasy, replacing the one we shattered. Regardless of any replacements, the old one must go.

I also have discovered that being awake can be as burdensome as it is liberating because now you know. Knowing comes with its own responsibilities and set of emotions and/or defenses it will evoke within you. For that reason, it is important to remember to be kind, fair, and realistic with yourself as you enter new levels of awareness. Understand that you are *not* going to become aware of it all. Considering the overwhelming number of issues needing to be addressed in the world, I think it is reasonable to say, all of us are failing someone just as, at any given time, someone is failing us.

For those who feel the awakenings they long for have been slow coming, you may be asking yourselves, "What am I doing wrong?" "Why have I not achieved the awakening I deeply desire?" However, for some, there are so many layers of life, memories, and mindsets in front of your awakening that the journey past the trail of thoughts, feelings and emotions is admittedly long and hard. I submit to you that persistence is the skill of the day.

Awakenings manifest when our choices meet meaningful moments in our life. These meaningful moments occur in our life due to a series of other meaningful moments that have occurred in our life. Our movement from one moment to the next moment with life happening in-between is what we have come to know as the "journey."

For all of us, the journey is impacted by circumstances within our control and circumstances outside of our control. Sometimes these life events can bring the happiest times. On the opposite end of that spectrum, they can bring devastation and unbelievable uncertainty.

Despite what is outside of my control, my focus remains steadfast on variables that are within my control. I can control my willingness to acknowledge when I am in need of a higher platform from which to live my life. I am in control of making choices that keep me moving in the direction of an awakening. Also, I am in control of my commitment to the pursuit.

Sixteen

A Call to Action

You don't need directions, just
point yourself to the top and go!

—Dwayne "The Rock" Johnson

There is a quote believed to have originated from an ancient Greek physician, Hippocrates. He said, "For extreme diseases, extreme methods of cure, as to restriction, are most suitable." From this quote the following saying was derived, "Desperate times call for desperate measures." More recently, I have heard a different version of the quote which says, "Different times call for different measures."

I think we all understand the thinking behind each of these sayings. But what is notable to me is not the thought that times would become desperate and we would not meet the challenge with a strong enough response. Neither am I excessively concerned that change would come, and we would fail to meet the challenge with an appropriate response. Although I value those concerns, my greater fear is that we would have an insufficient response to the issues that are already here.

Many of us are rushing at such a high speed that we are rushing past so much of what needs our attention. We are not aimlessly rushing. We are rushing for the sake of survival and all the elements we believe sustain our quality of life. We are rushing to be first, rushing to remain relevant, rushing to make sure we are one of the few who will get paid in a pot of limited resources, rushing to have influence, rushing to monetize our talents, and rushing to rest so we can rush back out and continue the cycle. We are rushing with purpose. The downside is that rushing makes it so much harder to pay attention to what is not directly in the trajectory of our present goals. But so much of what is outside of that trajectory is relevant to our journey, our perspective, and the story that will accompany us once we arrive at our goal. I get too busy to pay attention. I rush, too.

A few weeks ago, I took a moment to exhale and enjoy the most tranquil state I could possibly muster. I just sat, staring in awe at the sky as its majestic blue hue seduced me away from observing the land around me. This was the same sky I see every day. But this time I was paying attention. I discovered that birds actually play with one another in the air. They have a great sense of play. I knew birds were playful, but this was almost a full-on organized sport. How did I live this long and not know that? I learned how long a red tail hawk can hover stationary in one place. WOW! The physics of it are quite impressive. I learned how wonderful it can be to watch beautiful transformations of a lone snow-white cloud against a clear blue sky slowly floating overhead. From where I was sitting, on top of the Santa Monica mountains, it was unbelievable. It was so close. Moving slow and still fulfilling its purpose. Hmmm! Another lesson learned about what is possible.

The sky, birds, clouds: these are things we see every day. Yet, I was able to make so many wonderful discoveries about entities and elements I see so frequently that I no longer pay attention. This is not only what can happen with birds, clouds, and the sky. It also happens with people. We simply become too busy to pay attention. Some of those individuals may even be inside your household.

There is no need to feel down. It happens! It happens even when you may have the best intentions. The question is: How do we begin to make "paying attention" our new habit? The only difference on the day I exhaled is that I simply chose to view rushing as an option and as a short-term strategy. During the days prior, I viewed rushing as a necessity and a lifestyle that eventually became a habit. When I made that one shift in my perspective, suddenly I had time to pay attention.

As I said in a previous chapter, sometimes the hardest part about being empowered is remembering that you are. What we choose to do with our voice and our choice is not only about how it impacts "Y," it is also about how it impacts "X"—in other words, how it impacts you, your life, your happiness, your peace, your relationships, and your experience on this planet that we share. In many ways we have become too busy for "us." There is so much happening in the world around us. It is not that we do not care; it is that we often do not have time to get involved. We have learned to take comfort in and look to external systems to fill in and do what was always intended to be a natural extension of our relationship to one another. Just a normal part of life in this big village.

Just as the equation, "If X were true, what would it mean for Y?" does not need your permission to exist, so it is with the village. You do not get to choose whether you are in the village. The village exists. You are not here alone. The only thing we get to define is our role and contribution, which is, in essence, your story. Somehow, we have been led to believe that writing your story requires paper, printing machines, and a barcode. But your story is being written through your voice and with every choice you make every day.

In chapter one, I said, "I hope you will see that my stories are actually your stories, because there is some part of each story that is *our* story." I want you to know that your stories are also my stories, because there is some part of each story that is our story. It works both ways. As you learned through these pages, it was later in life that I discovered I was a writer. What I am now realizing is that at some level we are all writers! Every day we start with a new blank page hoping we will write a good one.

What we have always understood was that the basic tenets that kept the village thriving was the understanding and recognition of how much we need each other. There is no replacement for human interaction. Everything else that we institute is nothing more than a poor substitute for the heart, soul, perspectives, and dimensions we have to offer one another. There was a time when we understood that our answers would come from us. Then the answers moved to being someone else's problem. Now, we have actually convinced ourselves that systems will solve human issues that are emotional and not material. We have bought in to this notion so deeply that in some instances we are even allowing systems to raise our children. That was never the job of schools and foster care.

Even at their best, our systems are only faithfully watering the leaves. It is a noble effort. However, it does not change the reality that the uptake of nutrients happens from the roots. The leaves have no system for benefitting from what the roots are begging to receive. The roots are hard for systems to access, because the roots are planted in the soil that makes up the land that the village is built on.

There is one thing we as humans detest, and that is feeling bad about anything. Even when we know we have not chosen to be part of the cure, we never want to feel that we are part of the problem. This is especially true when the problem feels too big to fix. As humans, we tend to have an interesting response to these dilemmas. We respond with a type of "fight or flight." There are those that jump in and see no other option except to become part of the solution. Those are the ones who fight. Then there are those who take flight.

There is no need to summon any of your emotions in looking negatively upon either of the two responses. For many individuals their responses are defined by circumstance, not disposition. What does that mean? It means we have all been in both positions. None of us have responded to every cause, and none of us have walked away from every need. If I were to use any emotion at all it would be directed at those individuals who find comfort in not caring at all.

This is what I was speaking about when I mentioned dimensions and social categories. If you simply judge me based on the time when I took flight on an issue that is passionate to you, you may miss all the times I stayed to fight for issues that are passionate to me. Maybe your fight is against world hunger, and I am fighting the inappropriate labeling of minority children in schools, which was triggered by the biases of my child's second grade teachers. We spend so much time judging when we could be joining or even uplifting and inspiring. Why judge the fact that someone chose a different battleground? A battleground that you may have no interest in at all. Why refuse to acknowledge that it is a battleground, simply because it is different from the ones on your list of issues to address. Instead, why not celebrate the presence of another warrior? My son is no longer in second grade. We won that battle. Now I am available for a different battle of my choosing. Today, I am choosing to fight for "us."

Interestingly, there is a tendency I have observed that often occurs when the problem feels too big. We assume that those who are directly affected by the problem have the ability to or can learn how to acclimate, and they will survive. This is where our social categories become quite the lifesaver for us, not for "them." If I can see them as human in a different way than me, I do not have to give them credit for feeling pain like I do. If I can see them as a threat, I can justify all the ways in which my policies and practices hurt them or ignore their pain. If I can reside and interact just outside the range of their cry for help, I am not held accountable for being unresponsive to their plea.

Categories and classifications cloud our sense of civility and compassion. It clouds the best parts of who we are. This is not a request for you to develop an equation with the equivalence of $E=MC^2$, which would rightfully be perceived as being complicated. The equation I have been speaking about throughout these pages is as simple as remembering the village exists and recognizing that the role(s) you play or choose not to play matters!

I wish we measured our choices based upon cost. Not monetary cost, but human cost, emotional cost, intellectual cost. We have no idea how much we are losing, because we never truly understood the value of all that is sitting and walking among us. What I am trying to say is that the real national treasure is "us"—all of us. We are the hope we are waiting for. So, it all goes back to your "X," your voice, your choice, and what you are doing with yours.

If you think I spend time thinking and overthinking my life, then meeting me is going to be a big disappointment. This book does not derive from so many thoughts; it is manifesting from so many feelings and so many actions I want to take and want to see taken. I am craving small, powerful movements and simple, meaningful moments. A few weeks ago, for no reason at all and without much forethought, I sent an email to a complete stranger, just to say, "Good job." No, I do not spend an excessive amount of time analyzing my thoughts and actions.

However, what I am guilty of is formulating lots of questions. I have more questions to ask and unknowns to discover than I have life left to live or years to live it. But I am enjoying walking through my "in the meantime" with all my dimensions, in search of amazing possibilities.

The beautiful thing about having so many dimensions is that you do not have to give up one dimension just because you are calling another one forward. The warriors and role models that have influenced me are individuals who were equally wise, watchful, caring, compassionate, giving, assertive, adventurous, and fierce. Discovering the threads that bind us has been the wonderful part of our journey. This is a journey that is being fulfilled *despite* the existence of social categories created by others and *because of* my refusal to fit comfortably into the confines of ill-fitting categories others have created for me.

Since I have acknowledged that I have many questions, here is one question on which I often speculate: "Have you ever asked an eagle where they have been?" I desire to ask. I have asked. I have enjoyed hearing the answers. I will continue to ask. I often wonder what the world looks like from their perspective.

I can ask because I am not talking about birds. I am speaking of the eagles that walk among us. They are those individuals who have the wingspan and have honed the skill to fly at the highest heights, and yet, recognize when there is an issue great enough for which they must fight. They are not as rare as you may think. When you are rushing you may miss them. You might just need to slow down a little and pay attention. They are there. Some of them may have forgotten who they are over time and may need to be reminded. Some, as the old story goes, have been raised in coops with chickens and were never told they were eagles. Others know the unimaginable feeling of freely spreading their wings to soar.

My real desire is not simply to question eagles, but to increase my own altitude and see the world from that height for myself. Yes, I think that is what I will do. After all, it is my voice, it is my choice, I am empowered, and I own my "X." Why not choose to soar? As I acknowledge my desire to question and fly like an eagle, I also recognize the value of chickens and the importance of having the sweet sound of the sparrow, or the nectar-driven presence of the hummingbird. What I am saying is that the village needs "all gifts on deck."

I hope you will give yourself permission to speculate regarding the what-ifs and the if-thens. Throughout these pages I have been suggesting that some of our hypotheticals are real possibilities. They are within our power to bring into reality.

So, you ask, "What is my call to action?" I am calling everyone with wings to rise!

Be the change you wish to see in the world.

-Mahatma Gandhi

About the Author

Dr. Michelle Jackson-McCoy is a psychologist by degree and a writer and creative by sheer passion. She began her career lecturing at universities and directing research as a scientist. Dr. Jackson-McCoy has published in international journals and is a highly sought-after public speaker. Using her unique blend of art and analysis, she created a consulting firm that boasts a client list that included Fortune 500 companies, the entertainment industry, and governments. Consistent with her commitment to impacting positive change, she has raised millions of dollars to fund and create national models to restructure and revitalize institutions and communities worldwide. She is recognized nationally and internationally as one of the leading creatives and transformative thinkers of our time with an unwavering thirst for social impact. Being a mother of two sons has motivated her to do more. Today, she is owner of Bemont, an award-winning production company focused on social impact entertainment in all its forms. In this book, through the power of her gripping true stories, Dr. Jackson-McCoy opens her heart and her life to reveal her uniquely thought-provoking perspective about "us."

Acknowledgements

I want to extend a special thank you to those who have walked with me on this journey. I could not have accomplished this alone. This book is a product of a tremendous amount of love and support from family, friends, and a few strangers along the way. I am eternally grateful to those who dared to believe with me and believe in me.

To my sons Jackson and Antonio, who bring me the greatest joy, you know I love you. But what feels so incredibly amazing is how loved I feel by you. Thank you for your relentless support, encouragement, proofreading, and timely hugs. From the start of this book to the realization of this book feels like a lifetime to me, but it was a lifetime for you. Now, you are men making your own choices. Oh, how I love the choices you are making. I am watching you "become," and you are living your life with such integrity, distinction, passion, and always protecting your joy. Through the years, you have been unwavering in your support and generous with your expressions of love. Thank you for…just being you!

To my sister Sheila, my fierce supporter, you have held my hand every day of this journey. I have no words to express my gratitude for the privilege of living this life with you by my side. I realize that what we share is not ordinary and beyond words. So, I will not struggle to articulate what we have been blessed to enjoy together. You are one of the great gifts God has given me. I recognize the gift. I cherish the gift. Every day of my life I thank God for you my sister, my friend.

To my beautiful nephews Sam and Sean, thank you for always standing near. Your words of encouragement and gentle nudges have been priceless and greatly appreciated.

Finally, a special and immense thank you to all my unsung heroes who have been an invaluable source of strength. You see a moment and seize a moment to sow into someone else's life. You are rare jewels, and I will cherish you always.

Dr. Jackson-McCoy would love to hear from you!

Email:
contact@drmichellejm.com

Instagram:
instagram.com/dr.michelle.jm

Sign up to receive the latest updates:
www.drmichellejm.com

Also available as an ebook.

Made in the USA
Monee, IL
07 July 2026

56551555R00125